Ambulance Victoria

MICA Paramedic
Rapid Sequence Intubation

July 2009
3rd edition

Jeff Kenneally
Terry Marshall
Ian Jarvie

TABLE OF CONTENTS

FOREWORD

The Brain Trauma Foundation (BTF) has published guidelines for the pre-hospital management of patients with severe head injury (1). These recommend that the airway be secured as soon as possible after injury, and that endotracheal intubation (ETT), if available, is the most effective procedure to maintain an airway.

However, the BTF guidelines make no recommendation on which technique of intubation is the most appropriate. There is a range of techniques practised for intubation in patients with severe head injury in the pre-hospital setting. If airway reflexes are absent, intubation without drug assistance is possible. However, when trismus and/or a gag reflex are present, this approach has a relatively low success rate. In fact, there is now compelling data to show that outcomes are worse if patients with trismus or gag reflexes are intubated without neuromuscular blocking drugs (2,3,4).

Rapid Sequence Intubation (RSI) by paramedics is used in one aero-medical service in Australia (5) and some ground ambulance services in North America (6) in patients with severe head injury. However, clinical studies of outcomes using RSI have had conflicting results. For example, Davis et al. reported the effect on outcome after the introduction of RSI using case-control methodology (7). Overall, mortality was significantly increased in the RSI patients compared with control patients (33.0% versus 24.2%, $p < 0.05$). The reason for the increased mortality rate is uncertain, but may relate to low intubation success rates (86%), hypoxia during laryngoscopy, inadvertent hyperventilation and/or prolonged scene times following the introduction of RSI.

Alternatively, other studies have suggested that pre-hospital RSI improves outcomes in head injured patients. In the Pennsylvania Trauma Outcome Study, a subgroup of patients received RSI by aero-medical staff (2). The RSI patients had a decreased mortality rate compared with non-intubated patients. Bulger et al. reported a similar improvement in outcomes where RSI was used in a study in 1912 patients admitted to a trauma centre with severe head injury (8). When adjusted for baseline differences, patients intubated with RSI had a lower mortality rate compared with those in the no intubation group.

Despite the encouraging data, RSI has not been introduced into most ambulance services in Australia for a number of reasons, including cost of initial training, issues of skills maintenance and an absence of proven benefit. In particular, there is concern that failed intubation in the pharmacologically paralysed patient could worsen outcome or even prove fatal.

A prospective, randomised, controlled trial in Victoria has recently been completed. This study enrolled 312 patients over 4 years and will provide data to guide future clinical practice guidelines. Publication of this trial is expected in late 2009.

In the meantime, paramedic RSI has been authorised by the Medical Standards Committee of Ambulance Victoria for selected patients with neurological injury. This RSI Reference book is a core component of training to ensure that the procedure of RSI is carried out as safely and effectively as possible.

Dr Stephen Bernard MD
Medical Advisor
Ambulance Victoria

1. The Brain Trauma Foundation. Guidelines for pre-hospital management of traumatic brain injury. At www2.braintrauma.org/guidelines/downloads/ btf_guidelines_prehospital.pdf (accessed September 2005)

2. vWang H. Peitzman A, Cassidy L, Adelson P, Yealy D. Out-of-hospital endotracheal intubation and outcome after traumatic brain injury. Ann Emerg Med 2004;44:439-449

3. Brochicchio G, Ilahi O, Joshi M, Brochicchio K, Scalea T. Endotracheal intubation in the field does not improve outcome in trauma patients who present without an acutely lethal traumatic brain injury. J Trauma 2003;54:307-311

4. Murray J, Demetriades D, Berne T, Stratton S, Cryer H, Bongard F, et al. Prehospital intubation in patients with severe head injury. J Trauma 2000;49:1065-1070

5. Bernard S, Smith K, Foster S, Hogan P, Patrick I. The use of Rapid Sequence Intubation by ambulance paramedics for patients with severe head injury. Emerg Med 2002;14:406-411

6. McDonald CC, Bailey B. Out-of-hospital use of neuromuscular-blocking agents in the United States. Prehospital Emerg Care 1998;2:29-32

7. Davis D, Hoyt D, Ochs M, et al. The effect of paramedic rapid sequence intubation on outcome in patients with severe traumatic brain injury. J Trauma 2003;54:444-453

8. Bulger EM, Copass MK, Sabath DR, Maier RV, Jurkovich GJ. The use of neuromuscular blocking agents to facilitate prehospital intubation does not impair outcome after traumatic brain injury. J Trauma 2005;58:718-23

The first edition of this book was prepared in August 2002 to assist the introduction of Rapid Sequence Intubation (RSI) to the Mobile Intensive Care Ambulance (MICA) paramedics of the then Metropolitan Ambulance Service (MAS). This was to facilitate a prospective, randomised clinical trial investigating the value of pre-hospital intubation for the severely head injured patient. This trial was subsequently expanded to include three major population centres of Ballarat, Bendigo and Geelong, serviced by Rural Ambulance Victoria.

To participate in this trial and the RSI procedure, it was essential that MICA Paramedics were proficient in the practical skills and had a sound understanding of the principles involved in the RSI procedure. AS the RSI procedure is to be introduced throughout regional Victoria, these imperatives remain.

The introduction of RSI to the former Metropolitan Ambulance Service, and the selected areas of Rural Ambulance Victoria, were via the provision of educational information and skills practice at a Continuing Professional Education (CPE) day. MICA Paramedics then participated in and discussed the RSI process with an anaesthetist during an arranged in-hospital theatre placement. Accreditation was then gained following participation in an in-field clarification, review and assessment process. All three aspects were required prior to any authorisation to practice in-field RSI. For some MICA paramedics, the CPE day information has been provided either by the Monash University Department of Community Health & Paramedic Practice, the MICA 12 month post panel study day, or a Clinical Support Officer provided RSI Lecture.

Details of the Ambulance Victoria RSI accreditation process are outlined in the accompanying document 'Rapid Sequence Intubation – Accreditation Assessment' provided at the end of this book.

In August 2006, an appreciation of the collective experiences of the MICA paramedics of Ambulance Victoria (AV) and refinement of the RSI process and Endotracheal Intubation Clinical Practice Guideline (CPG) necessitated an update. A 2nd edition was published, which addressed these refinements and incorporated the experiential base that had been gathered.

Since the publication of the 2nd edition, the RSI trial has been completed, with the results in pre-publication by Dr Stephen Bernard and colleagues. A study of RSI for the Non Traumatic Brain Injured patients has also been conducted by MICA Paramedic Kate Cantwell and others, and is also in the pre-publication process. In addition, further refinements have been made to the Endotracheal Intubation CPG, and additional experiential trends have been gathered. In alignment with the anticipated introduction of RSI to all MICA paramedics in regional Victoria, it is timely for another update of this book.

The authors have taken the opportunity to enhance the content of various sections to attempt to add to the theoretical information. It is hoped to augment the readers understanding of the drug assisted intubation and associated processes.

Throughout this book various AV Clinical Practice Guidelines and Clinical Work Instructions are referred to. Be aware that these are the current versions as at the publication date and may change from time to time. Please ensure you refer to the most recent editions of these documents.

The book was designed to assist MICA Paramedics to increase their knowledge, understanding and practical performance of the procedure of RSI. It is intended to be used as a resource document in association with the MICA CPE – RSI handouts (or equivalent), the Novametrix Tidal Wave Sp User Manual, the Phillips MRx Monitor User Manual, the AV Clinical Practice Guidelines, the AV Clinical Work Instructions, and the RSI Video. It will be distributed to all participating AV MICA paramedics.

The first edition was formulated following consultation with the MICA paramedics of Air Ambulance Victoria (AAV) and incorporated their practices, and experiences of potential difficulties and techniques to avoid their occurrence. The second edition incorporated input from numerous sources, and particularly followed direct MICA paramedic experience. Similarly, in revising for this third edition, the authors have incorporated the further experiential base of the MICA paramedics of Ambulance Victoria.

Particular mention needs to be given to MICA Team Manager Paul Howells, for his considerable efforts in the production of the second edition.

The authors are appreciative of all assistance received from a large number of MICA paramedics and other sources in the preparation of this third edition.

May 2009

AUTHORS

- ➢ Jeff Kenneally   MICA Team Manager – Ambulance Victoria
- ➢ Terry Marshall   Group Manager Barwon – Ambulance Victoria
- ➢ Ian Jarvie   Clinical Support Officer – Ambulance Victoria

The authors wish to thank the following people for their specific assistance in the preparation and publication of this book.

- • Dr Andrew Bacon   AV Medical Adviser
- • Dr Stephen Bernard   AV Medical Adviser
- • Alan Gailey   AV Clinical Support Officer
- • Jon Hinton   AV MICA Paramedic
- • Paul Howells   AV MICA Team Manager
- • Dianne Inglis   AV MICA Paramedic
- • Colin Jones   AV Clinical Support Officer
- • Paul Stefaniak   AV Clinical Support Officer
- • Andrea Wyatt   AV Manager Clinical Education

3 PRE-HOSPITAL INTUBATION

Pre-hospital intubation is a controversial and much discussed subject. Airway management remains the priority in all medical teachings, from basic first aid through to the most advanced life support procedures. Though what constitutes 'airway management' remains controversial. Airway management to some is synonymous with intubation. However there are considerable other options short of 'the gold standard' that may prove adequate in the pre-hospital arena.

For the practitioner who finds intubation a necessary practice, a number of key factors need to be considered. The patients and circumstances encountered are almost always:

- Of uncertain diagnosis.
- Of unclear medical backgrounds, often of relevance to the paramedic.
- Non-fasted.
- Often have concurrent injuries and illness that both complicate and pose conflicting priorities.
- More staff may be required for optimum management than are often available.
- The paramedic has limited control over the situation or environment.
- There will often be great emotion and excitement from bystanders and family members.

Observation and research of pre-hospital RSI has identified a number of key areas that are essential if best possible outcomes are to be achieved. These include:

- Adequate pre-oxygenation.
- Ventilation to maintain preferred blood gas levels
- Maintenance of blood pressure
- Avoiding prolongation of scene times, to the detriment of competing priorities in management

The successful accomplishment of all pre-hospital intubations requires a structured and thorough preparation process, prior to the intubation attempt commencing.

During any assessment, management or manipulation of the airway and ventilation of any patient, some terms need to be understood by the paramedic.

Tidal Volume (Tv) is the total amount of gas moved into the lungs during each ventilation. It may be produced by spontaneous respiration. In this instance a relatively negative pressure (compared to the surrounding atmosphere) is produced in the lungs by the muscles of respiration, drawing air in. Or it may be produced by positive ventilation where gas is pushed in by external device. Combinations of the two are possible where positive support is added to spontaneous respiratory effort that proves inadequate in its own right. A normal adult tidal volume in spontaneous respiration is about seven mls / kg or 500 to 600 mls. The same adult requires around ten mls / kg tidal volume during manual positive pressure ventilation. The increased amount of the latter is to provide extra pressure to expand the chest without the assistance of the respiratory muscles. Tidal volume decreases with rest and sleep. It increases by as much as four times with exercise.

Dead Space is the amount of air that remains in the airways that is not involved in gas exchange. It includes the upper airway, trachea and bronchi. It amounts to around one third of normal tidal volume, or ~150 mls. Dead space is increased by anaesthetic / sedative drugs thus mandating increased oxygen concentrations in the inspired gases.

Alveolar Air is the tidal volume less the dead space within the airway. This amount varies considerably with oxygen demand. With greater muscle effort, more alveoli can be recruited increasing the reservoir available.

Minute Volume (MV) is the tidal volume multiplied by the respiratory rate over one minute. This is particularly important since the patient can alter the amount of gas delivered by changing either their tidal volume and/or ventilation rate. The paramedic should determine adequacy of both respiratory rate **and** tidal volume. Similarly, when providing positive pressure ventilation, the paramedic should consider both the rate and tidal volume provided each minute needs to be considered. This will vary with patient age, size and underlying presenting problem.

Functional Residual Capacity (FRC) is that volume of air left in the lungs at the end of normal exhalation. It includes the expiratory reserve volume that can be forced out with maximum expiration, and the residual volume that always remains. This varies with respiratory diseases that can increase or decrease lung volume. It can also be manipulated during assisted ventilation, including Positive End Expiratory Pressure (PEEP) and Continuous Positive Airway Pressure (CPAP) therapies. By manipulating the concentration of gases remaining in the FRC, the diffusion properties within the alveoli can similarly be altered.

Closing Volume (CV) is the volume of gas remaining in the lungs when the small airways begin to close during a controlled maximum exhalation. This is increased in obesity, late pregnancy, and COPD, especially when the body is supine. An increase in closing volume is reflected in the normal reduction in SpO_2 seen in supine obese or pregnant patients.

PATIENT ASSESSMENT

A sound base line is required for decision making and ongoing trend monitoring as early as practicable. Each patient will vary in regard to their main presenting problems and other factors that will compound any patient management. Attention should be paid to such management principles as pay-off and the AV Time Critical Trauma assessment guidelines.

- The initial patient assessment is the primary survey
- A comprehensive and accurate vital sign survey is mandatory. A determination of perfusion status, respiratory status and precise Glasgow Coma Score (GCS) is required.
- If suspected, a tension pneumothorax must be treated prior to any intubation attempt. A tension pneumothorax can significantly influence a patient's GCS, perfusion and respiratory status, and must be excluded.
- Continuous cardiac monitoring is required. The monitor should be positioned to maximise viewing with a clearly audible tone.
- Continuous pulse oximetry monitoring is also required. This should be positioned so that the airway paramedic, and assistant, can both visualise and operate the device.
- Assess a base line blood sugar level, to exclude a correctable cause.
- Assess a base line tympanic temperature. Patients in altered conscious states, those rendered immobile and those exposed to environmental conditions post-traumatic events may all have lowered body temperatures. This can affect assessment and be a factor in quality of patient outcome. Similarly, hyperthermic states may indicate environmental exposure or drug involvement.
- Good history taking should attempt to determine any non-traumatic causes of altered conscious state such as hypoglycaemia, drug overdose or cerebral event.
- A thorough secondary survey is required to establish the presence of other injuries that may affect management priorities.
- A traumatic injury pattern can produce concurrent time critical injuries leading to hypovolaemia, traumatic brain injury, chest injuries, increased time urgency and alterations in the effects of drugs used during intubation.

- Penetrating truncal trauma demands urgent surgical intervention. Patients with penetrating truncal trauma presenting with an altered conscious state and hypotension should not have scene times extended by Rapid Sequence Intubation (RSI). Expedient transport is imperative.
- Cervical collar application and good spinal care should occur early if the possibility of spinal trauma is suspected. Suspicions should extend to the elderly, where any traumatic mechanism exists, where any head injury is evident, where distracting injuries co-exist, or where there is drug or alcohol influence suspected.

5.1 HEALTH AND SAFETY

- Mandatory personal protective requirements include safety eyewear and gloves.
- P2 rated surgical masks should be worn. Airway procedures are high risk given the proximity to saliva, sputum and potential respiratory infective sources. In instances where infection risk is possible, including meningococcal and tuberculosis cases, surgical masks are mandatory.

6

AIRWAY ASSESSMENT AND INITIAL MANAGEMENT

Though a more generalised patient assessment has already been performed with some airway inclusions, a specific airway focussed assessment needs to be performed early. A thorough airway assessment will provide the foundation for all ongoing monitoring and management decisions. Without a sound foundation, errors in decision-making and management will be made. An airway assessment should look for normality, and therefore identify presenting difficulties, and suggest their early management priority. It is frequently suggested that poor or fatal patient outcomes can be attributed to initial airway obstructions. Similarly, an initial patient presentation can often be significantly improved with basic, or modestly advanced, airway management measures. These should always be explored before any advanced airway care ensues.

6.1 AIRWAY ASSESSMENT

Airway assessment is an absolute priority for any patient in an altered conscious state. It is partially undertaken during the primary survey, and continues in a more detailed and precise fashion during the vital sign and secondary examination.

- The patient in an altered conscious state should have an assessment for any gag reflex presence, with the **strict exception** of the traumatic or spontaneous head injured patient who is a candidate for RSI. The gag reflex helps protect against aspiration. An assessment can be made via an attempt to insert an oropharyngeal airway. If this is successful, cord visualisation under laryngoscopy should follow to inspect the upper airway more fully. Testing for gag can cause vomiting, which itself risks airway compromise. It can also lead to an increased intracranial pressure; an unwanted complication in any head injured patient.
- Evidence of upper airway obstruction should be sought. Look for stridor, hypoventilation, decreased breath sounds, increased use of accessory muscles of breathing, chest retraction and abdominal protrusion on breathing, cyanosis and / or diminished SpO_2. Always suspect an airway obstruction if difficulty in ventilation is found. Similarly, always suspect this if the patient has recently eaten.

- Look for evidence of airway trauma including:
  - Facial and neck injuries suggest a greater potential for intubation, and a greater risk of difficulty. Neck injury suggests difficulty in implementing cricothyroidotomy.
  - Facial burns, or having ash or soot evident in or around the mouth and nose, suggests a rapid deterioration is possible, with a possible need to intubate early. The need for intubation will need to be balanced very carefully with a reasonable time to get the patient to hospital.
  - Oedema of the upper airway suggests difficulty in implementing cricothyroidotomy.

The most common cause of upper airway obstruction is the tongue. Lateral positioning of the patient, jaw thrust techniques and insertion of oropharyngeal or nasopharyngeal airways may help.

Foreign bodies can be removed with lateral positioning, backslaps and the use of Magill's forceps.

Reflux of gastric contents in the unconscious patient is a passive activity and may occur without arousing the suspicion of the attending paramedic. Be alert for the smell of vomitus and the presence of vomit on face or clothing. All non-fasted patients should have the possibility of vomiting or aspiration suspected. If possible, early airway inspection under laryngoscopy is recommended. To assist in management, patients can be managed laterally, suction employed, cricoid pressure administered or Laryngeal Mask Airway (LMA) insertion or intubation undertaken.

Blood or secretions are frequently found, particularly in traumatic situations. Lateral positioning and suctioning can assist.

Laryngospasm is a temporary protective closure of the vocal cords that will pass after a brief period of time. If this occurs during any laryngoscopic visualisation or intubation attempt, return to gentle assisted bag and mask ventilation until it passes.

6.2

6.2 AIRWAY SUCTIONING

Prior to any attempt to manage an unconscious patient's airway, effective suction should be available as airway soiling is possible.

Suctioning attempts should be of minimal duration. Suction devices that run off oxygen driven venturi systems will exhaust the supply if used for long periods. Importantly, suction will remove air from the airway, cause delays in oxygenation / ventilation, and contribute to hypoxia.

Suctioning is best performed under laryngoscopy with a rigid suction catheter such as the Yankauer. Passive regurgitation found in the oropharynx will only be visible under laryngoscopy.

Where trismus is present, a soft suction catheter can be introduced into the cheeks. The soft posterior airway is delicate and easily injured by the blind introduction of hard catheters.

A soft suction catheter can be fed down the oropharyngeal or nasopharyngeal airway to provide suction. When suctioning through any airway device, the external diameter of the sucker should be less than half of the internal diameter of the tube to prevent negative pressure being applied to the distal airway.

Suctioning airways of patients that still have a gag reflex intact can lead to coughing, gagging or even vomiting. This can lead to elevations in intra-cranial pressure. This can also lead to vagal induced bradycardia and blood pressure changes.

Suction catheters can be reused on the same patient if suctioning the upper airway. If suctioning an endotracheal tube the catheter should be single use only. Suction should only be applied whilst withdrawing the catheter to minimise the impact of air removal from the alveoli.

If a suction catheter becomes occluded due to sputum or foreign matter, it can be dipped into a small container of water to encourage clearing the obstruction.

Infective and aspiration fluid should be suctioned from any Endotracheal Tube (ETT) as soon as practicable. The fluid of pulmonary oedema is slightly different. By lowering the pressure in the airway (alveoli), there is a worsening of the pressure gradient allowing additional inward fluid movement. Consider a brief upper airway only suction to assist visualisation during any intubation attempt; this is unlikely to be successful. Providing positive pressure ventilation can help provide resistance to fluid shifting, and maintain inflation of alveoli.

6.3 OROPHARYNGEAL AIRWAY

The oropharyngeal airway (OPA) is designed to keep the tongue from falling back and occluding the airway. It sits on top of the tongue and pulls it forward. It does not perform any other airway maintenance function and has no role in protecting against aspiration or removal of a foreign body.

It is more rigid than the nasopharyngeal airway. Once sited, the distal flange should sit just outside the lips.

Sizing of an OPA is important. They come in size ranging from neonate through to large adult. If the OPA is too long, it may injure or compress the epiglottis over the airway. If too short, it will not remove the tongue from being an obstruction. It is measured from the corner of the mouth to the earlobe.

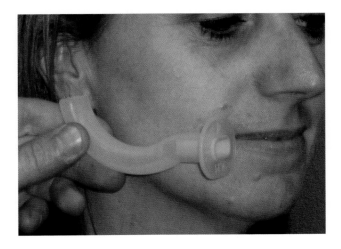

Suctioning can be performed by passing a soft catheter through the middle of an OPA.

An OPA is an unsuitable airway adjunct if there is a gag reflex present, as it can induce gagging and vomiting. It should not be forcibly inserted if the patient has trismus or jaw tone. Nor is it a suitable device in any conscious patient.

The oropharyngeal airway can be inserted alongside an ETT as a bite block. Unexpected, insufficient muscle relaxation can lead to biting. The ETT is soft, particularly once warmed in the mouth, and can be occluded if the patient bites downward.

6.4 NASOPHARYNGEAL AIRWAY

The nasopharyngeal airway (NPA) is similarly designed to keep the tongue from falling backward and occluding the trachea. It does not perform any other airway maintenance functions and has no role in protecting against aspiration or removal of foreign body.

It is softer than the oropharyngeal airway. Once sited, the distal flange should sit just outside of the nostril.

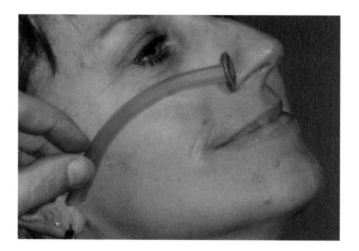

It is inserted into one nostril. Lubricate before insertion. If resistance is met, try twisting the NPA to continue progress. If unable to insert, try the other nostril.

Insertion of an NPA is perpendicular to the nose. Do not point the tip upward.

The end of the NPA sits in the posterior pharynx behind the tongue, often in line with the trachea. A soft suction catheter can be passed through the airway.

NPAs are less likely to induce a gag than an oropharyngeal airway and can be inserted despite trismus or jaw tone being present. The nasopharyngeal airway is tolerated better where a slight gag exists such as a drug or alcohol overdose. This also makes it suitable for trauma patients where an oropharyngeal airway is unsuited.

The devices are not suited where nasal injury or deformity is found. Nor are they recommended where base of skull injury is suspected, which makes their use in facial trauma limited. Unwanted passage through the fractured cribriform plate and into the cranial vault may follow.

6.5 THE DIFFICULT AIRWAY

During the initial airway assessment, the patient should be assessed for factors that might predict difficult intubation. Such factors include:

6.5.1 PATIENT PREDICTORS

Prominent front teeth will limit the ability to insert a laryngoscope blade into the mouth, and this includes a subsequent inability to move the blade. A reasonable mouth opening should accommodate three fingers width. Additional considerations, which may inhibit mouth opening include;

- A decreased ability to open the jaw creates similar problems to prominent teeth.
- The distance from the hyoid cartilage to the rear of the mandible is less than three fingerbreadths (<3cm).
- A decreased ability to move the neck. This will be the case when the patient has a degenerative disease of the spine and has lost flexibility, or there has been a traumatic mechanism and good spinal care has restricted movement
- Structural changes to the face and upper airway including angioedema, facial burns, facial trauma and epiglottitis.
- The patient with the short neck is often indicative of a difficult intubation.

The obese patient has the chest closer to the chin, making it more difficult to insert and position the laryngoscope blade. Ramping up the head and upper thorax to restore the line from the external auditory meatus and the suprasternal notch to horizontal will usually improve the view.

Similarly, the pregnant patient can be very difficult to properly insert the blade. Larger breasts can also make intubation difficult. Use of a shorter laryngoscope handle can assist, via removal and insertion of the blade, with a re-attachment once in the mouth can assist. Also, turning the laryngoscope handle at right angles towards the patient's right can assist; as the blade is inserted sideways into the mouth, slowly turn the handle back to the usual position.

The non-fasted patient may be considered a risk factor as it increases the likelihood of complications. However, all pre-hospital intubation patients will likely be non-fasted, and this should be assumed.

6.5.2 OTHER PREDICTORS

Not all contributory factors are patient related. Other extraneous factors need to be considered:

- An inexperienced practitioner
- Stressful circumstances including an emotional family or a paediatric patient
- An inability to place the patient in the best position. This includes trapped patients or those collapsed in small spaces. In these cases, consideration needs to be given to moving the patient to a better location prior to performing any intubation. This action will need to be weighed against the risks of patient deterioration during such delay and movement.

6.5.2

7 VENTILATION ASSESSMENT AND INITIAL MANAGEMENT

Whilst an initial airway assessment is the earliest priority, the next immediate main concern is early establishment of the patient's spontaneous ventilation efficiency. In the patient that will require assisted ventilation, the paramedic will need to consider all circumstances that may have an impact. The immediate implementation of supporting ventilation will require a considered and tailored response.

7.1 VENTILATION ASSESSMENT

The patient's spontaneous ventilation status should be re-evaluated as soon as the airway is cleared and patent.

If a re-breathing circuit is available, correctly place the mask over the face of the patient. A correct fitting mask should fit between the bridge of the nose and the middle of the chin. Various sizes should be available for differing sized patients, including neonatal through to large adult. The movement of a soft re-breathing bag can be used to visually, or via tactile sensing, assess adequacy of tidal volume.

A facemask should be placed on the patient regardless to assess the ability to gain and maintain an effective seal.

A thorough Respiratory Status Assessment (RSA) needs to be performed. This provides the most objective assessment of spontaneous respiration by evaluating visible and assessable physiological criteria. Together the elements of an RSA reflect the patient response, and hence effectiveness of respiratory effort.

Auscultation is a qualitative assessment, and can be unreliable. It can be difficult to correlate the sounds heard with adequacy of tidal volume. Auscultation should not be relied on, but rather considered as one part of a thorough assessment of ventilation.

7.2 ASSISTED VENTILATION

The aim of assisting ventilation for any patient is to try to either maintain or restore a normal ventilation cycle for the patient. The inspired air is comprised of numerous gases including oxygen, nitrogen, carbon dioxide and water vapour. The relative percentages are usually consistent, within normal atmospheric conditions.

During periods of patient physiological distress, the clinician can:

- Vary the concentration proportions of the inspired gases. Increasing the fraction of oxygen will increase the amount available to diffuse into the blood and be delivered to the tissues. Removal of unwanted gases (principally nitrogen and CO_2) from the inspired mixture means that any gas delivered will be of more immediate patient use during the crisis.
- Vary the ventilation being provided, regardless of the inspired gas supplied. The minute volume can be altered by variations in the ventilation rate and / or the tidal volume of each ventilation cycle.

Ventilation manipulation will not only assist with oxygen delivery, it will assist to manage pCO_2 levels. This is just as imperative as oxygen delivery, and poses its own problems for different patient managements.

During any ventilation assistance, close monitoring of pulse oximetry readings and end tidal monitoring will be required. Hand ventilation is unreliable for consistency in most patients, in particular trauma patients, and mechanical ventilation is preferred in these instances. For conditions subject to patient change, such as fragile respiratory illness, some degree of hand ventilation is useful to allow periodic adjustment of ventilation, as dictated by patient needs.

Either a self-inflating bag with the maximum available high flow supplementary oxygen attached, or an Oxysaver™ with the 100% oxygen re-breathing circuit, can be used. The **distinct preference is for a self-inflating bag** with the highest possible supplementary O_2 flow attached. If an Oxysaver™ is utilised, then an oxygen flow rate of 5–8 litres/minute is desirable. An effective mask seal is essential when using a self-inflating bag to ensure the exhalation valve functions correctly. At times, a second operator may be required to assist with providing an effective seal.

Oxygenation for at least 2 minutes is required to efficiently flush out nitrogen and to maximise the alveolar oxygen concentration and SpO_2. If necessary, the addition of Assisted Positive Pressure Ventilation (APPV) should be used during pre-oxygenation to ensure adequate tidal/minute volume and removal of CO_2.

7.3 DIFFICULT VENTILATION

Any difficulty in providing assisted bag/valve/mask ventilation must be considered before initiating an intubation attempt. Any such patient will become dependent on the effectiveness of the pre-oxygenation and management in any failed intubation situation. The inability to ensure adequate ventilation should be considered in advance.

Situations of difficult ventilation may include:

- Patients with facial hair/beards can be difficult to gain a proper seal on the facemask.
- Older patients can have sunken facial features or false teeth that have become dislodged or been removed. This alteration in facial structure can make it difficult to gain an effective seal.
- Obese patients can have fleshier faces and necks making it difficult to affect a seal and to hold the mask with one hand.

If the operator notices they are unable to maintain an effective seal or there is a requirement to replenish the oxygen supply with a rebreathing circuit, or an acceptable SpO_2 value (i.e. >92%) is unable to be maintained despite paramedic efforts, an assistant is required to assist with holding the facemask.

7.4 HAZARDS OF ASSISTED VENTILATION

APPV and Intermittent Positive Pressure Ventilation (IPPV) can lead to increased intra-thoracic pressure. This can produce a decrease in subsequent venous return (preload), leading to decreased cardiac output and blood pressure.

Any compromise in the blood pressure of any head injured patient will lead to adverse patient outcomes.

7.4.1 INTRATHORACIC PRESSURE AND HYPOTENSION

Patients presenting with problems of gas trapping, such as asthma, will be very sensitive to small intrathoracic pressure changes making the monitoring of assisted ventilation imperative.

In an asthma or Chronic Obstructed Pulmonary Disease (COPD) patient, and there is a decrease in blood pressure during APPV / IPPV, a problem solving regime must be quickly followed to correct the BP drop. This should include:

- Allow the patient up to one minute of apnoea to provide time for trapped gas to escape. Monitor pulse and SpO_2 throughout.
- If pulse and blood pressure do not return, assess the potential for a tension pneumothorax, and commence CPR.
- Administer a fluid bolus and /or inotrope support to increase venous return and cardiac output. If indicated, give consideration to the likelihood of hypovolaemia and the need to initiate appropriate fluid filling.
- Cardiac arrhythmias will also need managing, as per guideline.

The minute of apnoea is only for use where:

- APPV / IPPV has been administered and it is suspected that the patient has been hyper-inflated. This can happen at even normal ventilation levels. It should not occur with a patient who is spontaneously breathing without being assisted.
- Where there is a heart rhythm on the cardiac monitor that should be producing a cardiac output but is not. A bradycardic rhythm suggests extreme hypoxia and imminent cardiac arrest.

7.4.2 INTRAGASTRIC PRESSURE AND ASPIRATION

APPV and IPPV can lead to increased intra-gastric pressure by forcing air down the oesophagus, opening the cardiac sphincter and inflating the stomach. Usually ~ 20 cmH$_2$O pressure is required for this to occur, but this can become almost zero in cardiac arrest. The resultant gastric distension can:

- Reduce the movement of the diaphragm impairing ability to ventilate. This is particularly applicable to children who rely more significantly on their diaphragms to breathe.
- Lead to regurgitation of stomach contents increasing the risk of aspiration. This will remain an ongoing risk with children who often have uncuffed ETTs. This risk can be reduced by gentle backwards pressure on the mandible to reduce the size of the leak.

This distension can be prevented by the judicious application of cricoid pressure, noting that hard pressure on the cricoid can also obstruct the airway altogether.

Insertion of an orogastric tube is required to relieve the distension as soon as practicable. This shouldn't interfere with APPV / IPPV and would likely follow a successful intubation. The presence of an orogastric tube can interfere with an effective seal of the facial mask.

The orogastric tube or nasogastric tube should be measured correctly and marked for length with tape prior to insertion.

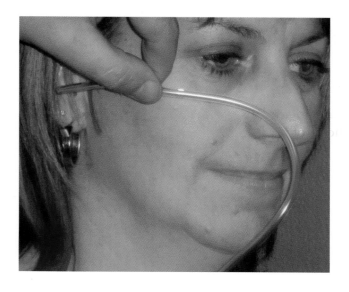

A large syringe should be available for gentle aspiration of gas in the stomach after placement.

A drainage bag should be available for ongoing drainage of the tube.

If the orogastric or nasogastric tube will not pass easily, it may have become curled up in the mouth. If this happens, it can be partially withdrawn and its passage recommenced and assisted into the oesophagus under laryngoscopy and with Magill's forceps. Additional measures can assist placement. These are moving the patient's chin towards their chest in non-traumatic circumstances, or via lifting of the larynx to increase oesophageal lumen size.

Examine the passage of the orogastric or nasogastric tube post insertion, to ensure that it has not entered the trachea and moved past the inflated ETT cuff.

Generally a 12FG tube suits up to 5 years of age, a 14FG up to 14 years, and then a 16FG accommodates 15 years of age and upward.

To confirm the placement, inject 20 to 50 ml of air into the orogastric or nasogastric tube, whilst auscultating over stomach. Gurgles indicate correct placement.

7.4.3 BAROTRAUMA

APPV and IPPV deliver positive pressures into the lungs, which presents as a risk for barotrauma.

In any patient where a pneumothorax is suspected, the introduction of APPV / IPPV substantially increases the likelihood of tension pneumothorax occurring. Management of tension pneumothorax is an urgent priority as soon as detected, and should precede any intubation attempt.

For patients needing increased lung inflationary pressures such as in a respiratory illness, the likelihood of barotrauma will increase.

7.5 TRAUMA

In trauma, a precise balance between oxygen delivery and carbon dioxide removal must be maintained. Adequate oxygen delivery must be provided, often by increasing the oxygen concentration delivered. A corresponding CO_2 removal must also be provided. This can only be manipulated by controlling the ventilation rate and minute volume.

In traumatic brain injury, the cerebral arterial vasculature is very sensitive to changes in the pCO_2. As CO_2 levels increase (hypoventilation), vasodilatation follows leading to an increased cerebral blood volume. This increases oxygen delivery but at the cost of an increased intracranial pressure. As CO_2 levels decrease (hyperventilation), vasoconstriction follows leading to a decreased cerebral blood volume. This reduces intracranial pressure but at the cost of reduced oxygen delivery and some local ischemia and lactic acidosis. Despite hyperventilation once being a normal management practice for the head injured patient, both outcomes are now considered undesirable.

7.6 RESPIRATORY DISEASE

The respiratory complications of heart failure, asthma, spontaneously or medically induced pneumothorax, and other diseases, will increase the level of airway resistance. This demands that increased pressure is required in IPPV or APPV to open the smaller airways.

Ventilation support allows for tiring muscles of respiration to rest before they fail completely. It also reduces a very high O_2 demand from those muscles and reduces the CO_2 production and lactic acidosis. However, not carefully applied will risk increased intrathoracic pressure, barotrauma and potentially decrease venous return and blood pressure.

7.6.1 HYPOXIC ILLNESS

The acute, respiratory distressed patient with a secondary hypoxic presentation has a minimal effective oxygen reserve to tolerate anything but the shortest apnoeic periods. Barriers to oxygen diffusion, including pulmonary oedema, aspiration and infection; all demand a higher delivery of oxygen concentration.

7.6.2 HYPERCAPNEIC ILLNESS

The acute, respiratory distressed patient with a hypercapneic presentation may have a slightly greater oxygen reserve than the hypoxic patient, although they will also be unable to tolerate anything but short apnoeic periods.

The conscious state will be more commonly affected by rising CO_2 than falling O_2, producing the characteristic 'glassy eyed stare'. A concurrent finding of an SpO_2 reading above 92% is not uncommon, even with loss of consciousness.

A decrease in SpO_2 in this group of patient implies impending respiratory failure and arrest. This must be addressed with urgency.

Correctly applied lateral chest pressure, to assist at the end of expiration, has anecdotally been shown to increase expired volume.

In these patients, normal minute volumes will potentially lead to hyperinflation. With this group, it is suggested to reduce the rate of ventilation during IPPV to 5 – 8 per minute. Ventilation rates can be titrated to maintaining adequate SpO_2 and blood pressure. CO_2 levels will be a lesser target factor, as they will very likely be high and to not be correctable in the pre-hospital time frame.

8 PRE-OXYGENATION

Increasing the oxygen concentration of inspired air increases the alveolar oxygen concentration through displacement of nitrogen. The increased concentration of O_2 in the alveoli leads to a greater diffusion gradient into the blood.

Pre-oxygenation of the patient is mandatory to increase functional residual capacity and tissue oxygen saturation. This helps avoid hypoxia prior to and during any apnoeic period that will occur during an intubation attempt. Hypoxia is clearly implicated in poor outcomes.

Pre-oxygenation should provide a sufficient oxygen reservoir to sustain the patient during the intubation attempt. An adequate oxygen reservoir will be less easily obtained where respiratory illness or traumatic injuries exist.

A normal oxygen facemask delivers a concentration of up to ~60% of oxygen at ~ 6-10 lpm. This is inadequate for pre-oxygenation prior to intubation.

Concurrent injuries in trauma, or a pre-existing illness that affects gas exchange, will need to be considered both for pre-intubation airway management, and the method and techniques of the intubation that will follow.

The monitoring of the patient's SpO_2 and $ETCO_2$ should be initiated during the pre-oxygenation phase, if either or both are not in-situ.

If the patient is being intubated using RSI, active ventilation should be stopped at the time of the administration of the initial paralysis agent (i.e., Suxamethonium) to avoid increasing gastric pressure and producing passive regurgitation of the non-fasted patient during fasciculation. If the SpO_2 is low, there is no option but to carefully continue to assist ventilation for 30-45 seconds until the Suxamethonium effect is noted.

9

PRE-EXISTING ILLNESS AND CONCURRENT INJURIES

Whilst co-existing injuries and / or illness will affect the ability of the patient to compensate for the effects of the Intubation Facilitated by Sedation (IFS) or RSI procedure and alter the effectiveness of any treatments provided. The patient's age will also be a factor in their response to the original insult, and the pre-hospital managements that are applied.

9.1 AGE

9.1.1 THE OLDER PATIENT

In all likelihood, the older patient may have some underlying illness and / or medications that can impact on the effectiveness of managing the airway, and the ventilation provided.

The older patient has a decreased elasticity of the lungs making it more difficult to ventilate.

They have a decreased ability to detect O_2 / CO_2 changes, via age related deterioration in their cardiovascular and nervous systems. Older patients may have already deteriorated considerably by the time they do collapse. The older patient will also have less effective gas transfer and transport mechanisms. They are also more likely to suffer more from lung disease, such as COPD.

Cardiovascular reserves are less with a decreased ability of the heart to compensate via increasing the heart rate and / or contractility. There is often a reduced blood volume. In the older patient, this may make lesser injuries more significant and drug effects more pronounced. These patients are more likely to have electrolyte and fluid balance disturbances. There is a reduced ability to compensate for illness, and any illness severity should not be underestimated.

Older patients are more likely to have reduced renal and liver function reducing drug metabolism, and potentiating drug susceptibility. Smaller doses of drugs are often indicated.

Some medications interfere with the actions or responses of several body systems, including the central nervous and cardiovascular systems. This will potentially impact on the clinical observations noted in some cases i.e. beta-blockers and heart rates. Recognition needs to be made during history taking, before making management decisions.

9.1.2 THE CHILD PATIENT

The child patient has a different set of criteria to consider when defining normal management, difficulties anticipated and urgency.

The child is not a small adult. They have a different body weight to surface area that dictates individual drug dose calculations for each child.

Differences in relative size of airway structures can be anticipated.

Similarly, the selection of airway and ventilation devices and techniques will need to be specific to the patient size.

Vital signs can be anticipated to vary dependent on age and weight, both in initial and ongoing assessment.

9.2 PRE EXISTING ILLNESS

9.2.1 RENAL FAILURE

Renal failure leads to multiple electrolyte derangements including hyperkalaemia. Any setting of hyperkalaemia is undesirable where Suxamethonium is to be administered, as there is a likely further potassium rise associated with fasciculation.

Renal failure may also interrupt the clearance of other medications or drugs, exacerbating or extending their effects.

9.2.2 MYASTHENIA GRAVIS

Myasthenia Gravis (MG) is a disease of the neuromuscular junction resulting in failure of nerve impulses to be properly transmitted and resultant respiratory muscular weakness and failure. It is a progressive disease and can progress very slowly over a long period of time. It involves a degeneration of acetylcholine receptor sites at the neuronal end plate. It is an uncommon patient presentation.

The disease can be graded into mild, moderate and severe presentations. The first should not significantly impact on paramedic management. The latter two require active consideration during any patient contact.

Benzodiazepines, including Midazolam and Diazepam, will affect nerve impulse generation and hence risk a decrease in respiratory effort. In paramedic settings, indications and doses should be changed from guidelines with reduced doses used. Depending on severity of illness, reduce the doses down to ¼ of the usual dose for the severe presentation. The likelihood of exaggerated respiratory failure should be anticipated.

Drugs that directly affect the neuromuscular action are of greater concern. Suxamethonium should be used in its usual indications and doses given its shorter action and it's 'switch on effect' at the end plate. Pancuronium, on the other hand, blocks impulse transmissions and has a much longer duration. The moderately affected patient, who is perhaps living with difficulty and being actively treated, should receive no more than half the usual indicated dose of Pancuronium. For the severely affected patient, no more than a one-quarter dose should be administered at a time. Monitor the patient closely for any further indications for additional drug doses.

9.2.3 OBESITY

The obese patient presents a number of anatomical complications for the paramedic to contend with.

The obese patient has a decreased period of tolerable apnoea. The mass of the patient will require increased ventilation pressures to expand the chest and move the diaphragm. There is a decreased functional residual capacity available and there will be a greater difficulty in maintaining adequate tidal volume due to increased airway resistances.

Providing a 'sniffing position' for ventilation may be more difficult. Some support under the shoulders ("ramping up") as well as the head may allow for improvement.

There may be difficulty in inserting a laryngoscope into the mouth, due to proximity of the chest and mouth. A pro-active option is to detach the blade from the handle, inserting it part way into the mouth, and reattaching. Usual laryngoscopy can then follow. Alternatively, if a short laryngoscope handle is available that could be used in preference. Also, turning the laryngoscope handle at right angles towards the patient's right can assist, and then as the blade is inserted sideways into the mouth, slowly turn the handle back to the usual position.

Ventilation of the obese patient will be more difficult due to increased pressures required and subsequent difficulty maintaining a seal.

There will be a greater difficulty in performing a cricothyroidotomy, with landmarks likely to be difficult to discern.

9.2.4 PREGNANCY

Though not a specific 'illness' as such, pregnancy brings its own peculiarities for consideration.

The pregnant woman can utilise the foetal/uterine circulation when in physiological distress. Fluid resuscitation should be implemented early and aggressively without waiting for signs of compromise.

When being maintained supine, the pregnant woman should be kept on a 15–20 degree angle to the left, to prevent the enlarged uterus from compressing the inferior vena cava. This can be achieved by padding under either the patients back or under the spine board.

The pregnant woman may present a difficult intubation in that both face and neck may be oedematous. It may be difficult to locate cricothyroid landmarks in a failed intubation.

Similarly, enlarged breasts may limit jaw opening and ability to insert laryngoscope blade. The blade may need to be removed from the handle and inserted before reconnection. Consider using a short handle if available. Turning the laryngoscope handle at right angles towards the patient's right can assist, and then as the blade is inserted sideways into the mouth, slowly turn the handle back to the usual position.

9.3 CONCURRENT INJURIES

9.3.1 CHEST INJURIES

Chest injuries can cause impaired gas exchange and difficulties in ventilation. This needs to be considered during the pre-oxygenation and post intubation phases of ventilation. Establishing an adequate oxygen reserve prior to intubation attempts may not be possible.

Hypoxia and hypercapnia will be more likely. All intubation attempts need to be short, with minimal apnoeic periods. Good preparation is essential to facilitate an efficient intubation attempt.

Initial alterations in conscious state may be influenced by impaired gas exchange and / or perfusion resulting from any chest injury. Good basic airway care and pre-oxygenation may overcome these.

APPV / IPPV, particularly after intubation, are likely to increase the development of a tension pneumothorax. A tension pneumothorax requires intervention as soon as one (or both) is recognised, even if prior to an intubation, and / or during any ongoing ventilation.

End Tidal CO_2 (ETCO$_2$) values may be altered if reasonably normal ventilation cannot be achieved due to chest injuries.

Pre-intubation signs of a tension pneumothorax include tachycardia, tachypnoea, decreased SpO$_2$, restlessness or gasping respiratory distress. Surgical emphysema is a good indicator of tension pneumothorax. A blood pressure drop and a loss of consciousness in the non-intubated setting are not reliable guides.

In the intubated patient, a sudden drop in SpO$_2$, a drop in blood pressure, tachycardia, neck vein distension and surgical emphysema appearance are strongly suggestive of tension pneumothorax.

9.3.2 BURN INJURIES

Burns injuries can lead to airway complications, dependant on the body area involved.

Facial and airway burns will present difficulties in gaining an effective seal to allow for pre-oxygenation and ventilation.

Airway destruction and the effect of toxic gases being inhaled into the lower airway may prohibit adequate ventilation and oxygenation and the establishment of an oxygen reserve.

Burn injuries, particularly if being treated with large intravenous fluid volumes, are likely to become oedematous. In the setting of airway and facial burns, it may be prudent to consider an RSI in patients with higher GCS scores than would normally be allowed for, to secure an airway before the patient deteriorates and intubation becomes more difficult.

Older burns beyond 24 hours will have electrolyte loss/shifting and a likely higher serum potassium. These will impact on pre-hospital drug therapy options. The use of Suxamethonium becomes contraindicated.

9.3.3 CRUSH INJURIES

True crush syndrome is likely to produce significant cellular necrosis and a subsequent increase in serum potassium, which will impact on drug therapy options.

Lesser crush injuries, where prolonged crush syndrome characteristics are not present, need to be assessed for extent of injury versus the likelihood of an increase in potassium release.

Patients found lying immobile for prolonged periods should be considered as having crush syndrome until proven otherwise, due to the extent of possible pressure areas and compromised circulation. An example will be the elderly stroke patient lying on the floor for a lengthy period.

9.3.4 HYPERTHERMIA

Hyperthermia is not in itself a problem in the setting of drug -facilitated intubation. It takes on significance in two particular settings, malignant hyperthermia and recreational drug use.

- Suxamethonium can be implicated in precipitating malignant hyperthermia. As a result of the drug administration, a severe elevated body temperature can shortly follow. This may be recognised by feel or tympanic temperature evaluation. It may also be recognised by a rising $ETCO_2$ not corrected by increasing ventilation. Use of this drug should be avoided where there is a known or familial history of such problem.
- Some recreational drugs can lead to increased metabolism and elevated body temperature. This crisis needs to be addressed urgently. Where basic care proves ineffective and the temperature remains high, the patient can be electively paralysed and intubated. The removal of all muscular activity can allow for a necessary reduction in body temperature.

9.3.5 HYPOTHERMIA

The hypothermic patient has a significantly reduced metabolism. The oxygen requirements are considerably reduced as are the production of metabolic waste, including carbon dioxide. As temperature decreases, the need for ventilation support similarly decreases. Ventilation parameters will need to be adjusted accordingly.

Further, drugs that are administered will also be metabolised more slowly. Their duration of effect will be longer, though the reduced body function may not make them more noticeably active. If actions from drugs are not observed, increasing dosage or administration rates is not likely to help.

Once a patient becomes moderately hypothermic, gentle handling and reduced drug administration rates becomes indicated (usually at double time intervals). Other usual procedures are performed. It should be kept in mind that as a patient is rewarmed, the usual expectation is that conscious state and spontaneous activity will similarly improve.

The severely hypothermic patient (less than 30 degrees body temperature) usually requires minimal intervention apart from protection from further heat loss and gentle rewarming. When they are required, therapeutic drugs are usually administered in one off boluses. Metabolism will be greatly slowed and so efforts to ventilate should be commensurately reduced.

Intubation in the severely hypothermic patient is usually unnecessary and often associated with increasing cardiac irritability. This has been shown to increase the risk of arrhythmias, including ventricular fibrillation. A lack of gentle handling may cause similar irritability.

Older burns beyond 24 hours will have electrolyte loss/shifting and a likely higher serum potassium impacting on drug therapy options. Use of Suxamethonium becomes contraindicated.

9.3.6 TRAUMATIC HYPOTENSION

A hypotensive patient undergoing an RSI process is at an increased risk of having the hypotension exaggerated. This is, in part, a result of the drug actions involved, and in part a result of the increasing scene times that are required to RSI the patient. As a result, strategies to address hypotension prior to the initiation of any intubation procedure are imperative, as are prophylactic strategies to avoid hypotension in the first place.

The traumatically induced hypotensive patient requires urgent surgical intervention. Uncontrolled bleeding, usually as a result of truncal trauma of any origin, will have the chances of a positive outcome diminished with longer scene times and the delay in reaching definitive care. Further, the drugs employed may exaggerate the hypotension and hasten poor outcomes. Both the vasodilating sedation drugs and the muscle relaxing paralysing agents have been implicated.

Where loss of consciousness is seen to be secondary to hypotension resulting from uncontrolled traumatic bleeding, the risk due to delay and the potential effects of RSI is considered to outweigh any potential advantage. In these instances a rapid transfer for surgical care, without an at-scene RSI should be the objective.

Where such rapid transport to surgery is not available, a reconsideration of the cost-benefit of intubation should take place. Such occasions may include:

- Long transport times due to an extended distance or a difficulty in extrication of patient
- An inability to provide adequate supportive personnel to maintain airway, ventilation, and other patient considerations
- Air transport considerations, where many procedures are not suited to in flight practice, or where patients must be rendered safe and fit for air travel

9.3.7

9.3.7 SEIZURES

Seizures immediately following a head injury are generally self-limiting. In a head injury where there has been a brief seizure, Pancuronium may be administered. Where seizures are pre-existing or not related to a head injury, no post intubation longer-term paralysis should be administered. The patient should be managed with sedation alone.

The preservation of the airway is always listed as paramount in any text on airway management, and the first priority in any resuscitation. There are several options available when implementing an airway management plan. These varieties of options need to be fully considered to allow a tailored plan that best suits the combination of patient and situation variables.

Reasons to consider intubation:

- Where there is a failure of more basic airway management techniques to provide a solution to airway protection.
- Where there is a need to provide ongoing airway protection, without a likelihood of an adequate patient improvement sufficient to provide airway self-maintenance. This becomes particularly applicable in the difficult conditions of ambulance transport.
- Where there is a need to provide ongoing respiratory / ventilatory support to ensure adequate oxygenation / ventilation.

Where there is a non-correctable failure of the patient gag reflex, intubation is a strong consideration. The considerations include:

- The transport time to get to a medical institution capable of providing advanced airway care.
- The experience and ability of the pre-hospital operator(s).
- Anticipated difficulty in intubating and ventilating the patient.
- The underlying concurrent problems with which the patient presents.

In regard to time to hospital, the intention is for intubation to occur as early as practicable. However, excessive scene delays and / or moving patients to the ambulance for intubation, followed by short transport times would seem incongruous. The increased difficulty of moving an intubated patient needs to be balanced with the minimal treatments able to be provided during any movement.

10.1 INDICATIONS FOR INTUBATION

Indications for intubation will include;

- Respiratory failure and respiratory arrest where there will be an ongoing need to provide ventilation support
- Cardiac arrest where there is no likelihood of immediate return of circulation and ongoing airway protection and ventilation support will be required.
- A loss of consciousness beyond that where the gag reflex remains sufficiently intact, and there is a likely need for ongoing ventilation. Usual indications include traumatic brain injury, hypoxic brain injury secondary to such event as post hanging, near drowning, prolonged seizure activity, drug overdose or post cardiac arrest.
- Traumatic and non-traumatic brain injury, where the need for airway control and maintenance of precise oxygenation / ventilation is required.

11 SCENE LEADERSHIP – ROLE AND TASK ALLOCATION

This section will specifically discuss preparations for drug-assisted intubations (IFS or RSI). However, the principles outlined should be applicable to all intubation attempts.

Though a drug-facilitated intubation should not be rushed, good time management and orderliness needs to be maintained to ensure an optimal outcome in the shortest reasonable time. Leadership and a clear role / task delegation are essential. Concurrent, effective delegation will lead to smoother preparation or management activity and will maximise scene efficiency. The minimum desirable requirement for a drug-assisted intubation is one intensive care (IC) paramedic supported by two appropriately trained paramedics. Two intensive care paramedics supported by two paramedics is strongly preferred.

11.1 TEAM LEADER / AIRWAY PARAMEDIC

The senior RSI qualified Intensive Care Paramedic should be the team leader.

The airway (intubating) paramedic should be the most skilled and best placed IC paramedic to intubate the patient. This should be irrespective of any role chosen prior to attending the case.

The airway paramedic should position themselves at the head end of the patient and layout all airway equipment within easy reach.

The team leader will co-ordinate the procedure and allocate tasks as required. They should take advice from others at the scene in any decision-making.

The team leader and the airway IC paramedic may be the same person.

11.2 AIRWAY EQUIPMENT PREPARATION

All potential airway equipment needs to be available, inspected and laid out prepared for use. It is important that equipment readiness is undertaken during the pre-oxygenation period for all intubation attempts. The paramedic performing the intubation should perform this role.

11.3 DRUG ADMINISTRATION

In most cases the second IC paramedic, if available, will be responsible for drawing up and administering the drugs. This offers the greatest level of teamwork and understanding. Effective communication between the drug and airway paramedic is essential. If the team leader is not performing the intubation, this is the role they should undertake.

This person should be placed by the IV access (usually a peripheral arm vein), with the drug container immediately adjacent. A free-flowing IV cannula (and required drugs drawn up) should be in place before **any** intubation attempt is made.

In some instances, single IC paramedics may delegate the drawing up and administration of the drugs, but this must be performed under their supervision.

Intravenous (IV) access must be obtained, pre-intubation fluid loading initiated and ongoing fluid resuscitation supervised. This can be delegated to a support paramedic. Pre-loading with fluid is essential.

It would be advantageous for the drug paramedic to be the person monitoring physical parameters. This enables regular monitoring of the pulse, blood pressure and SpO_2 values. The airway IC paramedic can be easily distracted. The drug paramedic should attempt to minimise these distractions by anticipation and being pro-active.

Effective management of drug preparation and administration is demanding; extreme care must be taken.

11.4 AIRWAY ASSISTANT

An airway assistant should be nominated to support the airway IC paramedic.

An airway assistant may be delegated the role of pre-oxygenating the patient prior to the airway IC paramedic taking over prior to the intubation attempt.

Cricoid pressure may be applied when instructed by the IC airway paramedic. The assistant should be briefed in this practice if required, and instructed not to release until directed to do so by the IC airway paramedic.

Support to the airway IC paramedic via providing suction equipment and bougie, second ETT, LMA, etc may be required. If two IC paramedics are in attendance, the drug paramedic is expected to become the assistant for the airway paramedic, after the intubation drugs have been administered. The second IC paramedic will be able to provide pro-active assistance to the airway paramedic during the intubation attempt.

11.5   OTHER DUTIES

Vital signs and SpO$_2$ monitoring should be continued throughout the procedure. Vital signs should be measured initially, immediately prior to the intubation, and soon after the procedure is complete. If there is delay in preparing, they should be re-evaluated for change. If the vital signs are of concern, such as in the hypotensive setting, they should be monitored with increased frequency.

Manual in-line cervical spine stabilisation should be provided during the intubation attempt if space and personnel are available. If personnel are unavailable for this, the intubating IC paramedic and the airway assistant should maintain an awareness of cervical spine stability and minimise head or neck movement during the procedure.

11.6 FUNCTIONAL INTRAVENOUS ACCESS

Large gauge IV access is preferred to allow for optimal drug delivery and fluid resuscitation. This is important given the possible side effects of the drugs involved in the procedure. A second IV site should be obtained to allow for unimpeded, ongoing sedation. However, this should not contribute to any delay in either treatment or transport of the patient.

The optimal site for an IV placement is the forearm where securing is more effective. The wrist and the cubital fossae are both prone to occlusion.

Ensure the intravenous fluid is attached securely and runs freely. Ensure a 'no needle' injection port such as a reflux valve or a 3-way tap is attached to the IV line.

If rapid volume replacement is required, a pressure device can be attached to the fluid bag. Manual 'squeezing' of the fluid bag may be used if personnel numbers allow.

Administer a fluid push of 10 mls / kg isotonic crystalloid (minimum 500 ml) to compensate for any drug-induced vasodilatation, and avoid hypotension. If IV fluid is indicated for other reasons, i.e., hypovolaemia, 20 mls / kg should be the initial target dose. Intubation is not to be delayed after the minimum amount is infused. This would not be applicable in the setting of fluid overload or pulmonary oedema, where avoidance of increasing preload is necessary.

Care and diligence are mandatory in the set up prior to any IFS or RSI attempt. If a waveform ETCO$_2$ monitor is not available in working order, no IFS or RSI procedure should be commenced.

If possible, connect the capnograph into the ventilation circuit during the pre-oxygenation period to ensure correct functioning and to establish a baseline ETCO$_2$.

All capnograph readings should be preceded by at least six ventilations, to obtain an accurate reading and waveform.

The capnograph and cardiac monitor should be positioned to allow both the airway paramedic and the team leader or support intensive care paramedic to visualise them continually.

The airway paramedic should mark the position of the cricothyroid membrane on the patient's neck.

All vital sign readings including pulse, blood pressure and SpO$_2$ measurements need to be regularly monitored during the procedure and all participants made aware of any adverse trends.

12.1 AIRWAY PARAMEDIC PREPARATION

The airway paramedic is required to layout the following for potential immediate use, prior to commencement of any intubation attempt.

- Have a clean and suitable sized surface available to lay equipment out on. A pillowcase or towel folded in half to the right side of the patient's head is appropriate. This isolates the preparation area, and is an indicator to others at the scene to remain clear.
- Test and have effective suction at hand
- A self inflating bag connected to the maximum available high flow oxygen source (or a rebreathing circuit such as the Oxysaver)
- Connect and inspect the capnograph to the bag/valve/mask system. Similarly connect pulse oximetry. Ensure monitoring is visible.
- Layout all failed intubation equipment including bougie, nasopharyngeal and oropharyngeal airways, LMA and cricothyroidotomy kit. It is not necessary to open the LMA or cricothyroidotomy kits but they should be present and with all equipment necessary for use.
- Orogastric or Nasogastric tube

- Colourmetric CO_2 Detector (Easy-Cap)™ for fallback.
- Have two functional laryngoscope handles available, ideally one a short variant.
- Have at least two laryngoscope blades available, with a larger size if needed.
- Have two ETT available including one of a smaller size.
- Have all ancillary equipment available, including stress reliever, cuff inflator and stylet.
- It is suggested the selected ETT have tie off tape pre attached at the estimated lip length, and an introducer be inserted with small 'J curve' applied at the end. Lubricate the ETT tip. If desired, a 10 ml syringe of air may be attached to the ETT to allow for cuff inflation.

Connect relevant ventilation and $ETCO_2$ monitoring equipment in the following order:

- ETT
- 150mm extension tube (stress reliever / liquorice stick)
- Bacterial filter
- $ETCO_2$ connections
- Self inflating bag

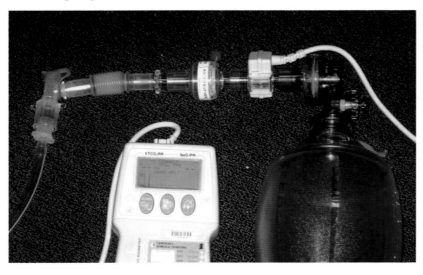

Any Colormetric 'Easy-Cap™' device should only be used in the event of failure of the capnograph, **after** the intubation attempt has been completed. It must not be used as a planned substitute for the capnograph during the intubation.

12.2 DRUG INFORMATION AND PREPARATION

To avoid an inadvertent drug administration error during any drug facilitated intubation process, as many safeguards as are reasonable should be adopted to verify each drug and dose. Each drug should be in a different size, standardised syringe with the drug ampoule attached for clear identification. Each drug ampoule should be read and verbally checked with another paramedic for the name, dose and expiry date. **All drug syringes need to be clearly labelled** with an identifying 'sticker'.

Sedation must precede the paralysing agent administration to avoid paralysing a still partially aware patient. This can lead to patient distress and cause detrimental changes in intra-cranial pressure (ICP).

12.2.1 FENTANYL CITRATE

Fentanyl Citrate is a narcotic used in the drug facilitated intubation context to provide sedation to blunt any awareness the patient may have of the procedure and of being intubated.

The onset of action is almost immediate, with a duration of up to 60 minutes. Fentanyl is the first sedative administered due to this speed of onset, and its associated analgesic activity.

A **100mcg /2ml** (1 ampoule) is drawn up into a **10ml syringe** with one ampoule attached. Fentanyl can be diluted to 10ml with normal saline to make half dose administration more accurate.

The standard full dose is 100mcg.

The dose is reduced to 50mcg if the BP is < 100mmHg systolic, or the patient's age is above 60 years old (or in traumatic brain injury a heart rate of > 100 / minute). This is to avoid the cardiovascular effects of the drug.

If the patient's BP (or heart rate) returns to normal values during the preparation, continue with the 50mcg dose. These patients are fragile and more susceptible to subsequent drug effect. This is a one off dose, so no further ampoules will be required after the initial bolus.

Fentanyl can display the central nervous system depressant activity of depression, respiratory depression and reduced spontaneous ventilation. It can also cause diaphragmatic and intra-thoracic muscle rigidity, which may affect ventilation.

Unwanted side effects should not be reversed with naloxone, as the sedation effect is imperative in the intubated and / or paralysed patient.

12.2.2 MIDAZOLAM

Midazolam is a benzodiazepine used in the drug facilitated intubation context to provide sedation to also blunt any awareness the patient may have of the procedure, being intubated and in maintaining the placement of the ETT. The onset of action is from 1 minute, with a duration of 20 minutes.

A **15mg** ampoule is drawn up into a **20ml syringe,** with the ampoule attached. This should be diluted to 15ml with normal saline for a solution of 1mg per ml.

The presentation of Midazolam may be in either **5mg / 1ml** or **15mg / 3ml** ampoules.

Pre-calculate the dose to be given and the volume of solution represented by that dose.

Enough Midazolam will remain to allow for at least one subsequent 2.5 to 5mg bolus of drug to assist in maintaining intubation.

The standard full dose is 0.1mg / kg to a maximum of 10mg.

The dose will be 0.05mg/ kg if BP is < 100mmHg systolic, or the patient's age is above 60 years old (or in traumatic brain injury a heart rate of > 100 / minute). In traumatic head injury, if the BP is <80 mmHg, the bolus dose of Midazolam is 1 mg. This is to avoid a potentially catastrophic cardiovascular collapse.

If the patient's pulse or BP returns to normal values during the procedure, continue with the 0.05mg / kg (or 1 mg) doses. These patients are fragile and more susceptible to subsequent drug effect.

Midazolam is the second sedation agent administered, due to its primary sedation, longer onset time and respiratory depressant activity.

Midazolam may be used as the sole sedation agent post ETT placement, via bolus IV doses.

12.2.3 SUXAMETHONIUM CHLORIDE

Suxamethonium is a short acting, depolarising neuromuscular relaxant drug used to produce deep muscular relaxation and paralysis to facilitate intubation. The onset is within 45 seconds, and it will wear off within 4 – 6 minutes. It allows for a balance between the time to perform the intubation, and the non–ventilating period, if the intubation attempt is not successful. Suxamethonium is the only available drug that provides the necessary timing combination.

100mg / 2ml (1 ampoule) is drawn up into a **3ml syringe,** with the ampoule attached to the syringe.

This gives a concentration of 50mg per ml for the delivery of 1.5mg / kg of drug. In practise, the dose administered will be 75, 100, 125 or 150mg to the closest 25mg. Round upward if required as per the following table.

Weight / kg	Dose / mg
50	75
60	100
70	125
80	125
90	150
100	150
> 100	150

The maximum dose is 150mg.

If more than 100mg is required, draw up two syringes as per above instruction and **NOT** into one syringe. This is to avoid administering excess paralysing agent.

A functional waveform capnograph **must** be used if Suxamethonium is to be administered.

Following administration, fine muscular fasciculation may be observed for a short period. These are due to the initial depolarisation of the skeletal muscles, before synaptic blocking and paralysis occurs. There may be no visible fasciculations observed. The cessation of any fasciculation is an indicator of the onset of muscular paralysis.

12.2.4 ATROPINE SULPHATE

Atropine is an optional drug that is required only when specifically indicated. It is a vagal blocking, anticholinergic drug that aims to increase the SA and AV node and hence heart rate. Its onset is less than 2 minutes, with a duration of up to 6 hours. It is indicated in the RSI setting wherever heart rates are found to be in, or may drop into, a bradycardic situation. In the paediatric setting, Atropine is given routinely regardless of finding of bradycardia.

Draw up **0.6 mg /1ml** (1 ampoule) into a **1ml syringe,** with ampoule attached.

It must be drawn up regardless if initial heart rate or blood pressure, as the paralysing agents can produce an excessive acetylcholine like effect that leads to bradycardia. The sedation agents also have possible cardiovascular side effects.

Atropine is to be given if, or as soon as, the heart rate drops below 60 / minute, irrespective of perfusion and blood pressure. It is administered to protect cerebral perfusion by assisting with blood pressure maintenance, and to prevent an excessive bradycardia from developing.

A single dose of 0.6mg is to be given.

If the heart rate remains < 60 / minute after 0.6mg of Atropine, it is unlikely the drugs administered for the IFS / RSI will be the cause of any bradycardia. Reassess and look for an alternate cause, i.e. tension pneumothorax, hypoxia, or hypovolaemia. If the pulse continues to remain at < 60 / minute, continue with any intubation procedure.

If the heart rate drop occurs several minutes after the sedation or paralysis drugs are administered, it is also unlikely the drugs are responsible. The possible alternate causes need to be considered.

Some settings of RSI may provide for bradycardic presentations initially, particularly the cerebral event. Though this is expected, Atropine is still indicated prior to the RSI.

12.2.5 PANCURONIUM BROMIDE

Pancuronium is a non–depolarising neuromuscular relaxing drug administered to produce deep muscular relaxation and paralysis to maintain placement of ETT. The onset of action is 2 minutes, with a duration of up to 45 minutes.

The presentation of Suxamethonium and Pancuronium are similar. To avoid inadvertent administration of the incorrect paralysing agent, Pancuronium should **not** be drawn up until the ETT placement has been confirmed by capnography and capnometry. A failed intubation in the setting of a longer lasting paralysing agent may be potentially fatal.

The standard dose is **8mg (2 ampoules of 4mg / 2ml),** drawn up into a **5ml syringe**, with the ampoule attached.

There is no fasciculation associated with Pancuronium administration.

Although the nominal duration of Pancuronium is 45 minutes, actual duration of paralysis will be patient dependent and routine monitoring for signs of muscle activity is required. Further doses of Pancuronium may be required if any sign of muscle activity returns.

Pancuronium was the initial choice of longer-term paralysis agent in Ambulance Victoria due to its blood pressure maintenance action, which was considered beneficial in traumatic brain injury.

12.2.6 ALTERNATE PARALYSIS AGENTS

Ambulance Victoria guidelines allow the use of Suxamethonium and Pancuronium as the paralysis agents of choice.

Other agents are available, and may be encountered in ED / ICU or inter-hospital transfer settings. A summary of some of the alternates is as follows.

Atracurium; has an onset of 2–3 minutes, and a duration of 25–45 minutes, which is not dissimilar to Pancuronium. However, the muscle relaxation of Atracurium will wear off at a quicker rate than Pancuronium. Atracurium may also cause bronchospasm or hypotension via histamine release – particularly in patients with prior cardiovascular disease. Unlike Pancuronium, Atracurium has no vagolytic activity, and will not lead to a tachycardia.

Cisatracurium; has an onset is 2–3 minutes, with a duration of 50–60 minutes. The recommended dose for intubation is 0.15 mg / kg, which would be a complicated calculation in the pre-hospital environment. Cisatracurium is an analogue of Atracurium, and histamine release is also a factor.

Rocuronium; has an onset is 1–3 minutes, and it has a duration of 30–50 minutes. The suggested dose is same as Suxamethonium for RSI. Rocuronium does not have the tachycardia side effects of Pancuronium. There appear to be no major complications of this drug that are more disadvantageous than Pancuronium which suggest it may be a suitable alternative for longer term muscle relaxation in the pre-hospital arena.

Vecuronium; has an onset of 2–4 minutes, and a dose dependent duration of 30–60 minutes. It does not lead to the tachycardia that Pancuronium does, due to less vagolytic activity, and has essentially no cardiovascular side effects. It comes in powder form and requires reconstitution. Whilst not a major issue, from the pre-hospital point of view this would add an unnecessary complication to what is already a significant procedure.

12.2.7 MORPHINE SULPHATE

Morphine is the narcotic of choice for longer-term sedation by infusion. This is consistent with in-hospital practice, and will permit smoother patient handover and ensure continuity of care.

It is less potent, has a slower onset and a longer duration than Fentanyl. It also has a larger effect on the cardiovascular system than Fentanyl. These traits combined make it the lesser alternative for the preparatory sedation for intubation purposes.

Morphine can be used as the initial intubation sedation, but should only be used in the absence of Fentanyl. If it is used as the initial sedation, the dose will be 0.1 mg/kg, with a half dose of 0.05 mg/kg for the patient over 60 years old, has a blood pressure of <100 mmHg, and in traumatic head injury has a heart rate >100 / minute.

It should be used in conjunction with Midazolam for longer-term infusion sedation, as they provide a good combination of analgesia, sedation, and amnesic activity.

12.2.8 CRYSTALLOID FLUID

Fluid volume therapy, using isotonic crystalloid solution, is indicated both before and after any drug-facilitated intubation. The vasoactive sedation drugs used can affect a patient's blood pressure, and pre-loading of volume is mandatory. It is also indicated post the drug administration to maintain blood pressure.

An initial preload of 10ml/kg is indicated prior to any drug administration to compensate for anticipated vasodilatation/hypotension. A minimum of 500ml is required.

If a patient is hypotensive prior to intubation, a more aggressive fluid push should occur.

If a patient's BP is low initially and corrected by fluid or other means, the drug-assisted intubation is still to be carried out with reduced doses of the sedation drugs. The cardiovascular effects of the drugs administered may precipitate a profound response.

To maintain and/or restore blood pressure post drug administration large volumes (>40ml/kg) may be required. This is particularly so where concurrent injuries exist.

13 HEAD POSITIONING AND LARYNGOSCOPY

Not all intubations will proceed uneventfully. The intubating paramedic, and their assistants, will need to be well positioned and make well-judged decisions to maximise intubation success. Consideration of the airway manipulation options during the preparation phase will enhance the chances of success.

13.1 AIRWAY PARAMEDIC POSITION

The usual position for the paramedic providing airway care is behind the head of the patient with the patient supine (occasionally laterally). Thus all visualisation and techniques will be performed with the patient 180 degrees to the intubating paramedic.

Optimal positions are often not available to the pre-hospital operator. Difficulties with patient placement are frequent. Regular occurrences include positioning on the floor, in vehicles, in the outside environment and of being confronted by a variety of unfavourable atmospheric conditions. The ambulance environment is usually cramped with little room for movement, correct layout of equipment or assistance.

Kneeling on one knee with the other upright is a common choice. Conversely, the operator can kneel on both knees or even lay prone facing head to head with the patient.

If basic airway difficulty is confronted, such as an inability to clear fluid or apply cricoid pressure, airway care can continue in the lateral position. Intubation can still be performed. The operator needs to conceptually think through a 90-degree rotation.

Patients trapped in traumatic situations may not be able to be moved from the position found. The airway operator may need to sit in front of the patient and apply airway techniques facing the patient. In this context, the laryngoscope can be inserted in an 'ice pick' fashion with the lower jaw pulled downwards and forward rather than lifted. Conversely, if access is available, intubation can be achieved by standing over the top of the patient. This can be physically difficult to achieve and is less suited to shorter paramedics.

13.2 PATIENT POSITION

Most patients will be managed in the supine position during the performance of advanced airway procedures. This will usually be the chosen position of care for ongoing ventilation. Basic airway care suggests lateral positioning to assist with drainage/removal of fluid and foreign bodies as well as to cause the tongue to fall forward and away from the airway. Most airway techniques can be performed in the lateral position.

Similarly, ventilation can be provided laterally. Ventilation is usually taught on CPR mannequins that remain supine, with lateral positioning not a concept commonly embraced. The non-intubated unconscious patient being positive pressure ventilated is a high-risk candidate for aspiration.

The trauma patient with spinal care is best-managed supine with the head in the neutral anatomical position.

The pregnant patient should be managed with a 20-degree tilt to the left, rather than supine, to avoid uterine and foetal inhibition of the great vessels reducing venous return.

The pulmonary oedema patient can be intubated sitting up with a slight recline on the ambulance stretcher.

The usual best position for all airway care is the 'sniffing position'. This is best achieved by the placement of about 4cm of padding beneath the occiput with the patient supine.

This is acceptable for the spinal care patient where it is encouraged to return the head to a neutral anatomical position. This position is suitable for both the insertion of an LMA or a cricothyroidotomy. It also assists in providing a good glottic view for the operator. A greater view of the anterior larynx is provided. The laryngeal view is diminished with both flat posturing and a backward head tilt.

Once in the 'sniffing position', a gentle backward pull on the upper jaw can increase visibility even further creating a straight-line view down to the cords. Neck flexion can cause partial flattening of the trachea increasing ventilation difficulty. The 'sniffing position' minimises this.

The patient with severe osteoporosis may not be able to be placed into an alternative airway position. Instead, this patient may have to be managed in the position found with pillow/padding support placed under the head in that position.

The patient in respiratory failure secondary to acute pulmonary oedema can be intubated with the patient kept in the sitting position. Supine positioning of such patients can lead to dramatic fluid accumulation in the oropharynx, obscuring any view and leading to cardiovascular collapse from increased preload.

13.3 ENDOTRACHEAL TUBE CHOICE

The largest tube size suitable for each patient should be selected. The ETT inside diameter will be smaller than the patient's airway; this increases the airway resistance, work of breathing and ability to move gas. This is particularly problematic for COPD, asthma and other patients with obstructive airway problems. Too small an ETT selection will compound these problems. This must be balanced against attempting to place too large an ETT that will not fit between the vocal cords.

Generally, a large adult accepts a 8.0mm ETT, and an adult female or smaller adult male or teenage male a 7.0mm ETT. Some subjective judgement is required.

The paediatric sizing formula for ETT selection is (Age/4) + 4.

Any intubation attempt should have a smaller size ETT immediately available.

13.4 LARYNGOSCOPY

13.4.1 LIGHTING

Lighting is rarely optimal for a pre-hospital intubation. Bright external light can diminish visibility under laryngoscopy. This can be minimised by;

- Ensuring the globe brightness is maximised with new globes and batteries before use. A thorough pre-shift equipment check is required
- Covering the airway paramedic and the patient's head with a blanket to remove the outside lighting

13.4.2 BLADE SELECTION

Though there are many varieties of laryngoscope blade and size, options for paramedics are usually more limited.

The most common adult blade variety is the curved Macintosh, which accommodates the shape and size of the tongue and oral cavity. It has a side flange to allow positioning of the tongue to the left of the oral cavity, and permit an unobstructed view of the vocal cords. Size ranges from the neonatal size to the largest size 5, which is rarely used. The usual choice for an adult would be a size 3. The tip of the Macintosh blade fits into the vallecula in most patients and encourages good technique when used. The size 4 can be fallen back to in the larger adult or difficult intubation. Longer length blades can encourage use as a fulcrum, rather than proper technique.

The Miller straight blade is usually intended for the paediatric use. It relies on a different technique suited to the anatomy of a child less than 3 years of age. There is an adult sized blade but the technique for use is of lesser value in all but the large epiglottis settings. The tip of the Miller blade goes over the top of the epiglottis, approaches the glottic opening, and lifts the epiglottis upwards to provide a view.

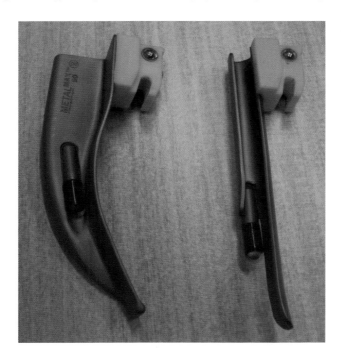

13.4.3 TECHNIQUE

The curved Mackintosh blade is inserted on the left side of the mouth and follows and compresses the tongue before ending in the vallecula groove. A gentle force is then applied perpendicularly along the line of the handle to allow for visualization of the cords.

Occasionally, the blade can be inserted beyond the vallecula without inserting into it. This will see the epiglottis trapped by the blade and obscure the view of the vocal cords. The handle of the laryngoscope will likely be very close to the mouth with most of the blade in the mouth. If this is suspected, withdraw the blade part way back out, gently angle the blade tip up into the tongue and slide in again seeking the vallecula.

The straight Miller blade technique is different. The blade is inserted alongside the tongue down the right side of the mouth. The vallecula is not aimed for but rather there is a deliberate intent to trap the epiglottis. A lesser force is required to bring the vocal cords onto view. This best suits the child anatomy and the larger epiglottis. It is easy with this technique to insert the blade too deeply or to damage the gentle airway structures being pinned.

13.4.4 AIRWAY GRADING

Visualisation of the vocal cords is an inherent component of airway inspection during laryngoscopy. Due to anatomical variances, the vocal cord view may range from a complete, unobstructed sighting to no view of the cords at all.

It is essential to assess the vocal cord view during the early stages of an airway inspection; this will guide the intubating paramedic in the approach that needs to be taken. Airway assessment and vocal cord view need to be assessed after blood, vomitus and secretions are cleared, and patient position is optimised.

In 1984 Cormack and Lehane[1] described a vocal cord viewing classification scale, for use in the teaching of intubation for pregnant patients. The scale is from one to four, with one being a complete, clear view, and four with no view of the cords.

If a one or two grade view is sighted, the first intubation attempt should proceed with the expectation of a successful attempt.

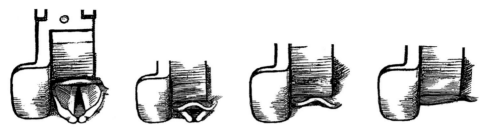

If a grade three or four view is sighted, the airway bougie should be immediately used.

Cormack – Lehane Classification (1984)			
Grade 1	Grade 2	Grade 3	Grade 4

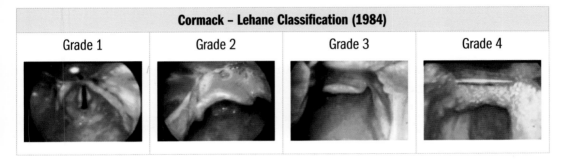

An alternate assessment method is the Mallampati scale[2]. This involves the assessment of tongue size relative to oral cavity size and degree of uvula view, and is a score to assess the potential difficulty of intubation. The Mallampati scale also uses a one to four score, with one as the best view, and four as the most restricted. As an assessment using the Mallampati scale involves oral cavity visualisation, its pre-hospital use in the urgent setting of an IFS or RSI is limited.

Another indicator of potential intubation difficulty is the thyromental distance. The thyromental distance is from the upper edge of the thyroid cartilage to the chin, with the patients' head fully extended. If this is less than 6 cm, or the length of the mandible is less than 9 cm, a difficult view of the vocal cords should be anticipated as an anterior larynx is indicated. This may be a reasonable guide for some pre-hospital patients; however the trauma patient would provide an exception due to the necessity to minimise head extension for possible cervical spine injury avoidance.

13.5   ADJUNCTS TO LARYNGOSCOPY

The vast majority of airway views will be grade one or grade two on the Cormack–Lehane scale. The paramedic must take care to not grade the view without using proper positioning or adjuncts. On occasion, the view will not be so easily achieved, and these occasions will not always be predictable. A set of adjuncts should be routinely available to assist;

- Laryngeal pressure can be used to assist with bringing anterior cords down and into view. This is most useful in the trauma setting.
- Utilisation of cricoid pressure may minimally assist with similarly altering the vocal cord view.
- Use of an introducer stylet to help direct tube insertion.
- Use of a airway bougie to assist with the actual intubation, where an effective laryngeal view cannot be achieved.

A different blade size is an option. A larger size can reach further into the oral cavity, if that is the problem, and can allow greater leverage. This leverage can lead to a poor technique 'fulcrum' effect, risking dental damage to the patient.

If a cervical collar has been fitted, it will need to be undone prior to any intubation attempt to allow for jaw opening and access to the cricoid area. The cervical collar will need re-application following successful intubation, and the securing of the ETT.

In the trauma patient, the described 'sniffing position' should not be altered. In other settings it can be desirable to lift the head further into an exaggerated 'sniffing position' further improving the view. This may require use of a pillow with the head lifted two or three times the usual amount to achieve the ideal horizontal line connecting the external auditory meatus to the lowest point in the suprasternal notch.

13.5.1 LARYNGEAL PRESSURE

This is the deliberate manipulation of the larynx during laryngoscopy to bring the glottic opening downward from a difficult anterior view. It is known as Backwards, Upwards, and Rightwards Pressure (BURP) given the direction of manipulation[3].

It can be applied concurrently with Cricoid pressure. Once applied to improve the laryngeal view, it may need to be kept on during the entire intubation attempt Laryngeal pressure should not be confused with cricoid pressure.

13.5.2 OPERATOR LARYNGEAL MANIPULATION

This is basically the use of the intubator's right hand during any intubation attempt to manipulate the larynx to experiment with facilitation of the vocal cord view. Once a preferred view is obtained, the operator asks the airway assistant to take over holding the larynx in that position. This is really a variation of laryngeal pressure with operator input.

13.5.3 CRICOID PRESSURE

Cricoid pressure is also known as Sellick's manoeuvre. It is primarily used as an airway protective technique, though it has some use as an adjunct to laryngoscopy. The theory is the oesophagus is soft and unsupported, as compared to the trachea and its cartilage rings. By pressing down on the hard cricoid cartilage, the oesophagus can be compressed and occluded whilst maintaining tracheal integrity[4].

Airway structure movement can vary with the application of cricoid pressure; this may or may not improve the vocal cord view. A common error is to unintentionally apply more force with the thumb, and this moves the larynx away from the airway assistant and out of the line of sight of the airway paramedic.

Variation of performance limits its effectiveness. The actual pressure being applied can be uncertain. An ideal pressure would be sufficient to 'blanch' the skin of the fingertips being used.

It should **not** be applied during any actual vomiting given the risk of tearing the oesophagus during opposed peristaltic motion.

It is generally applied either early in the unconscious, gag-less patient or concurrent with drug administration in the drug-facilitated intubation.

An airway assistant will apply the cricoid pressure. This person needs to be trained in the application of cricoid pressure if they are not familiar with it.

Once commenced, it must remain applied until the airway paramedic has secured the airway to ensure there is no risk of subsequent aspiration. The airway paramedic must advise when it is safe to remove cricoid pressure.

Cricoid pressure must be removed to allow for the correct insertion of an LMA, where the tip sits behind and below the cricoid ring.

13.5.4 INTRODUCER

The introducer stylet is a malleable metal rod that can be placed inside an endotracheal tube. This assists with:

- Maintaining the semi rigidity of an ETT as they can become soft and floppy once inside the warm patients' mouth or in warm atmospheric conditions.
- An ETT will normally only be able to be 'steered' in the direction of its length. The stylet can be bent to allow the ETT to be directed into otherwise unable to reach places. If the bend is too great, there will be difficulty in feeding the ETT off.

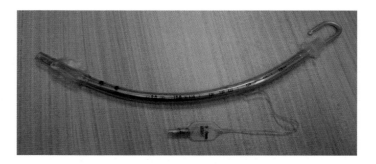

The end of the stylus should not protrude past the distal end of the ETT. When the end is at the desired point, the operator end is bent over to ensure that it cannot travel any further into the tube. This is not an airway bougie; it should not be used to locate the trachea and have the ETT railroaded over it. Lubrication of the stylet will avoid any undue 'sticking' to the ETT, and assist removal.

There are a variety of different sized stylets to suit paediatric through to adult ETTs.

The stylet can be routinely used, though they should only be used on the first attempt. If a subsequent attempt intubation is required, the airway bougie should always be used.

If a stylet is used, the tip of the ETT should be lubricated to facilitate easier passage.

13.5.5 PLASTIC AIRWAY BOUGIE

This is a malleable rod softer and longer than the introducer stylet. It is designed for positioning directly into the trachea, whether unsighted or not.

It is ideal for use in the failed intubation setting and should be used routinely on any second attempt to intubate. It can be used routinely for any attempt.

One end of the airway bougie is angled upwards about 30 degrees approximately 20 – 30 mm from the end. This can be inserted into the oropharynx, allowing it to be angled upward into the anterior area when the vocal cords are not visible on laryngoscopy.

It is placed into the trachea. Once positioned, the feel of the cartilage rings can be felt rubbing against the tip. The operator needs to hold the bougie in place until the ETT is properly placed.

Given the need to hold the tip in position, and the significant length of the airway bougie still protruding, great care must be taken by the user to avoid eye injury. It is preferable to continue the insertion with an assistant.

The ETT needs to be placed over the airway bougie to allow insertion. It can be fed on prior to the intubation attempt or once the tip is positioned. The ETT can then be slid down the bougie using it as a guide wire. Known as 'rail-roading', the ETT is then positioned into the trachea to the usual length and the bougie removed.

If any resistance is encountered during passage of the ETT, the ETT can be twisted 90 degrees anticlockwise to allow the angled tip to move past the vocal cords.

The airway bougie comes in adult and paediatric sizes.

14 RAPID SEQUENCE INTUBATION

RSI is an intubation with the rapid administration of a drug regime, in a specific order, to facilitate the placement of an ETT. The following is an explanation of the steps required.

14.1   INDUCTION AND INTUBATION

Maintain continued vital sign monitoring throughout the procedure with SpO_2, $ETCO_2$ and cardiac monitoring. Vigilance is required. An assisting paramedic can be assigned to this task.

If not already positioned, the airway paramedic should now move to the patients' head and take over bag / valve / mask for a short period immediately prior to the intubation attempt.

Agreement should be communicated, from and to, all paramedics that all preparations are complete and the procedure is to commence.

14.2   DRUG ADMINISTRATION

As the RSI name suggests, drug administration is in sequence and in a closely spaced (rapid) period of time. The sedation drugs are administered first. To allow them enough time to be effective first, wait 10 seconds before administering Suxamethonium. The same principle applies for IFS, without the paralysing agent.

Fentanyl should be administered prior to Midazolam. Fentanyl's onset of action is more rapid than Midazolam. Midazolam will have a greater effect on spontaneous ventilation and therefore should be given after Fentanyl.

In the RSI procedure, sedation is not administered primarily to assist with the insertion of the ETT. Sedation is to blunt a normal anxiety / sympathetic response and to render the patient unaware of their paralysis. In IFS, the sedation drugs are not supported by muscle relaxants, so are required to also facilitate the passage of the ETT.

Sedation may diminish vascular tone and reduce BP. However the patients' anxiety, pain or other natural physiological responses to their insult may cause an accelerated heart rate. If the heart rate is >100 / minute, but BP is normal, standard doses of sedation are appropriate. **Except** in Traumatic Brain Injury (TBI) where reduced doses of sedation are required to avert a potential significant reduction in blood pressure. An elevated heart rate should be considered an indicator of a sympathetically maintained BP.

Suxamethonium will paralyse to facilitate the intubation.

Flush in all drugs with a generous fluid bolus.

It is important to avoid hypotension at all times during the drug assisted intubation procedure.

14.3 APPLICATION OF CRICOID PRESSURE

Apply light cricoid pressure during the administration of the sedation drugs, and firm pressure after the Suxamethonium is administered.

14.4 ASSISTED VENTILATION

This should be ceased at the time of drug administration. Continued APPV can push gas into the stomach, increase intra-gastric pressure and lead to regurgitation. If a high pulse oximetry reading, and hence an adequate oxygen reserve, is not attainable, IPPV should continue carefully until the intubation attempt begins.

Cricoid pressure should not be released until the airway paramedic declares the ETT correctly positioned and confirmed by $ETCO_2$ monitoring, the cuff inflated and ETT secured. This minimises any risk of aspiration into the lungs.

14.5 FASCICULATION AND SIGNS OF PARALYSIS

Fasciculations are fine motor muscle movements caused by Suxamethonium induced depolarisation. There will be no fasciculation observable during an IFS attempt.

Look for fasciculation signs after the Suxamethonium administration. Fasciculation signs may vary from none observed through minimal to vigorous. Other personnel during the procedure can look for fasciculation signs in other parts of the patient.

The airway paramedic should confirm paralysis using other signs including a loss of jaw tone, motor activity cessation, and the absence of spontaneous ventilation.

Intubation should be possible after fasciculations are observed, or 30 – 45 seconds after drug administration.

14.6   COMMENCING INTUBATION

Intubation prior to adequate sedation or paralysis should never be attempted.

The traumatic closed head injured patient will have lost cerebral autoregulation reflexes; therefore, will be unable to control Intracranial Pressure (ICP). Raised ICP will have adverse cerebral consequences. Proceeding without adequate sedation or paralysis will lead to a sharp rise in BP due to a laryngeal stimulation reflex, with a consequential rise in ICP. The ICP rise will continue for a significant time despite removal of the laryngeal stimulus.

15
ENDOTRACHEAL PLACEMENT AND CONFIRMATION

Once a cessation of fasciculation is observed (or an appropriate time has elapsed) in an RSI (or jaw tone / trismus has relaxed in an IFS) laryngoscopy should be commenced.

The grades of laryngeal view must be assessed during the intubation attempt using the Cormack – Lehane 1 to 4 scale; with 1 being a full cord view and 4 no view at all.

The grading should be assessed as the best view obtained following suction and airway manoeuvres.

A grading of 3 – 4 should indicate immediately moving into the difficult / failed intubation drill. This should prompt use of the bougie for any further attempt. The airway assistant paramedic will need to be alert to this occurrence and be prepared to assist as required.

A reasonable intubation attempt time frame should be within 15 seconds.

Visualisation of the cords and passage of the ETT during intubation is a helpful but not wholly reliable placement guide. It is easy to lose sight of the ETT tip at the last moment and still misplace insertion. It is not relevant in the difficult intubation.

Many ETTs have an International Standards Organisation (ISO) mandated black line above the cuff. This should be just visible above the vocal cords to reduce the chances of a right main bronchus intubation.

Once passed, the ETT should be held by the airway paramedic, and pinched between two fingers on the same hand whilst grasping the patient's jaw. It should not be released until suitably tied in to avoid inadvertent misplacement.

Perform the Oesophageal Detector Device (ODD) test with the cuff deflated, and before any post ETT ventilation. The trachea is supported by cartilage; the oesophagus is not. Pulling back on the plunger will cause the oesophagus to collapse and make it difficult to keep pulling.

- Withdraw the plunger back to approximately 40ml. A free withdrawal of 40ml of air is indicative of a tracheal placement.
- Difficulty withdrawing the plunger and complete or nearly complete retraction suggests an oesophageal placement.
- Free withdrawal of plunger to 25-40ml but with subsequent retraction 10 to 15ml suggests a right main bronchial intubation. Withdraw the ETT slightly and recheck. It may also indicate vomitus in the airway, other airway obstruction, or be caused by obesity.
- The ODD is accurate for paediatric patients over 1 year old. The amount of air withdrawn is reduced to 20 mls from 1-5 years.

If oesophageal placement is indicated via ODD, do not withdraw the ETT. Instead, proceed to $ETCO_2$ for definitive assessment of placement. Record the result of the ODD result in documentation as ODD oesophageal, ODD Tracheal, ODD Equivocal or ODD Fluid.

Inflate the ETT cuff after the ODD test, with the recommended amount of air, as per the ETT manufacturer's instructions.

Use a bacterial filter to protect the $ETCO_2$ adaptor from moisture and secretion. Attach the bacterial filter to the stress reliever (liquorice stick), and then to the $ETCO_2$ adaptor, which is connected to the ventilation device. Confirm the capnograph waveform and ETT placement after at least six ventilations. If the correct waveform is not present, recognise the ETT is oesophageal and follow the difficult / failed intubation drill without delay.

Continue with all other standard checks:

- Tracheal squash test (right main bronchus check). This is important to ensure the tip of the ETT is not resting on the carina and is not too far displaced down one bronchus. This would result in improper inflation of either lung[5].
- Auscultate the chest in the standard positions over left and right lungs to confirm air entry and ETT placement. This can be difficult if the patient is still spontaneously breathing, as may be the case in IFS. In this case, they will have audible air entry throughout even if the ETT is incorrectly placed.
- Auscultate over the abdomen to listen for gurgling and look for distension.
- Look for bilateral equal expansion of the chest. This test is unreliable in many settings including overweight patients, pregnant women and large breasted women. Movement of the stomach when the oesophagus is intubated can also produce a degree of chest movement.
- ETT misting is unreliable. This effect may be caused by water vapour in the stomach. An absence of tube misting is likely to be indicative of an oesophageal placement.
- The feel of a soft bag is completely unreliable. It is possible to have some reinflation effect from air in the stomach.
- Look for skin colour improvement of the patient.
- Look for improving SpO_2
- The presence of gastric contents is suggestive of oesophageal placement but can indicate aspiration
- Carbonated drinks can produce an $ETCO_2$ reading in the short term. Connect the $ETCO_2$ device and assess the reading after at least six effective ventilations.

Adequately secure the ETT. ETT tape is preferred secured to the ETT with a clove hitch knot at the level of lip placement. The ETT should be held secure until it is tied in securely. A proprietary device can be used as an alternative to ETT tape.

15.1 POST PLACEMENT PROCEDURE

The ETT should only be secured once you are confident it is placed correctly in the trachea.

Note the length of ETT at the lips. The tube should be at the point where the cuff (if present) is just through the cords. Too shallow and the cuff may damage the cords or the end will be easily displaced. Too deep and you risk intubating one bronchus. Be mindful of oedematous lips impacting on the 'lip length' estimation, and if this is a factor, noting the length at teeth is a viable alternative.

Adult males are usually 21 cm at the lips, smaller adult males and adult females are 20 cm at the lips, and smaller adult females and larger children 19 cm at the lips.

For children use the formula (age / 2) + 12 cm.

Re-check the ETT position periodically and after every patient movement. Gently adjust the length if required.

It is important to insert a bite block to reduce the risk of an inadequately paralysed patient biting on the soft ETT. An OPA, or an alternative proprietary device, are the preferred methods.

Once the ETT has been unequivocally confirmed with $ETCO_2$ waveform monitoring, and secured, administer Pancuronium promptly to ensure an overlap of effect with the Suxamethonium.

Insert an orogastric tube or nasogastric tube, and remove any trapped air / pressure from the stomach that may interfere with ventilation. This is important post IPPV and essential for children.

Re-check all monitoring parameters of $ETCO_2$, SpO_2, cardiac monitor, pulse and blood pressure. Document accordingly.

16

POST INTUBATION CARE

Connect to appropriate ventilation as soon as practicable. If using a self-inflating resuscitator, ensure that it has the oxygen reservoir in place on the inlet side, and is connected to the maximum available high flow oxygen source.

16.1 VENTILATION OF THE INTUBATED PATIENT

Ventilate at 10ml/kg and ~12 ventilations per minute. **Avoid hyperventilation as this leads to poorer patient outcomes.**

The tricyclic drug overdose patient is an exception to this principle. In this setting there is a deliberate attempt to induce a respiratory alkalosis. Under these conditions the drug action is reduced considerably. Ventilate at 10ml/kg and increase the ventilation rate to reduce $ETCO_2$ as per guideline. This will likely be in the 20–25mmHg range.

Similarly, Diabetic Ketoacidotic (DKA) patients should be ventilated at a rate consistent to maintain approximately the $ETCO_2$ they are initially found with. This patient will have a respiratory alkalosis in response to the underlying metabolic acidosis. Any attempt to maintain usual or normal $ETCO_2$ values will compromise this and compromise the pH further. This patient should similarly be hyperventilated.

The asthmatic patient is also managed differently. This patient has a reduced ability to exhale and risks gas trapping at normal ventilation levels. Ventilate instead at 10ml/kg and 5 – 8 ventilations per minute. A high $ETCO_2$ value in the asthma patient is to be expected, and tolerated.

Don't compromise good ventilation in pursuit of target values on monitors that may not be achievable or may be misleading due to concurrent injuries or pre-existing disease. Trends can be more important than actual numbers. However, ideal values for the traumatic brain injured patient are SpO_2 >95% and $ETCO_2$ 30 – 35 mmHg. Similarly, respiratory distressed patients may normally tolerate slightly lower SpO_2 and higher $ETCO_2$ values.

It is imperative to maintain adequate ventilation throughout the entire pre-hospital care period, both before and after ETT placement. The airway paramedic should supervise the ETT and ventilation. At all times this must be concurrent with all vital sign and electronic monitoring.

16.2 EQUIPMENT MALFUNCTION

Inspection and checking of equipment prior to any procedure is mandatory. Equipment failure can lead to difficult and stressful situations for the IC paramedic. Their complete is clearly the preferred position.

All equipment should have a back up or alternative available before proceeding. This would include a selection of laryngoscope blades and handles along with all disposable items, such as endotracheal tubes.

The most critical pieces of equipment should all have a redundancy. The provision of a second capnograph would be advantageous in the event of first device failure, although this is unlikely in the pre-hospital scenario. If not available, a chemical CO_2 detector, i.e., the Colourmetric Easy-Cap™ must be available before any drug facilitated intubation occurs. The IC paramedic should be familiar with the $ETCO_2$ device(s) available and understand how to change batteries and reset factory default settings as part of a problem solving regime.

In the event of an inability to effectively ventilate the patient, a problem solving algorithm should be followed:

- Is there an inspiratory gas leak? The ETT cuff may be damaged. In the short term, push the chin down on the chest to affect a workable seal. At the earliest opportunity, replace the ETT. To assist with this, consider inserting an airway bougie inside the existing ETT and use it similar to a guide wire.
- Is there difficulty ventilating? Inspect for circuit leaks or hose kinking in any rebreathing circuit. The pressure release valve may also be open in a rebreathing circuit; check all connections and hose linkages. Consider changing to an alternative ventilation circuit if the problem cannot be resolved. Bacterial filters that become moistened also increase effort of ventilation, and may need replacement.

16.3 BACTERIAL FILTERS

Bacterial filters (as they are referred to in AV), will also provide protection from moisture, secretions, and possible viral particles.

A bacterial filter should be in line to protect the $ETCO_2$ adaptor from moisture. Be aware these will reduce gas flow very slightly in normal use. Once moistened with secretions or aspirant, gas flow may be significantly reduced.

Signs of difficulty would include visible secretions around the filter, reducing SpO_2 values and increasing $ETCO_2$ not correctable by increasing ventilation. If filter soiling is suspected, replace the filter.

Inspect the side stream cap on the filter. It must be securely in position. If it is not, the $ETCO_2$ reading will be adversely affected, producing a 'leaking' waveform on capnography.

16.4 ETT SUCTION

Aspirant or secretions in the ETT will reduce flow and interfere with gas exchange. If it is suspected at any stage, the ETT should be suctioned periodically. A small amount of saline solution can be used down the ETT just preceding suction. This is to loosen secretions for easier removal.

Oxygenation with at least several ventilations should occur prior to any suction attempt so as to minimise potential apnoeic effects.

A clean flexible suction catheter should be used on each suction occasion. Though not an aseptic procedure, cleanliness should be a priority.

The suctioning removes oxygen and decreases alveolar pressure as well. Only apply suction whilst withdrawing the catheter to minimise this impact.

All personal protective equipment (eyewear, gloves and facemask) should be worn during this procedure. Other paramedics and assistants should be advised to be clear to avoid inadvertent contact with secretions. Place the suction catheter straight into an appropriate disposal bag.

16.5 MONITORING ETT PLACEMENT

Continually monitor ETT placement to ensure that it does not become either displaced from the trachea or pushed into the right main bronchus.

16.6 OROGASTRIC TUBE

A distended stomach containing gas from APPV or food / beverage can put pressure on the diaphragm. This will impact on the ability to expand the chest during ventilation. This is particularly important for paediatric patients.

When convenient, place a large bore lubricated orogastric tube and aspirate stomach contents. For the paediatric patient, it is imperative to insert an orogastric tube as soon as practicable. Not only are children more susceptible to diaphragmatic embarrassment, paediatric endotracheal tubes are not cuffed removing the effective seal provided for adults. The usual size of an orogastric tube is for a 12FG up to 4 years of age, a 14FG over that with the option of a 16FG for normal adult size.

If the tube does not pass easily into the oesophagus, laryngoscopy and Magill's forceps can be used to assist its passage. If insertion of the orogastric or nasogastric tube remains difficult, additional measures can assist placement. These are the placing of the patient's chin towards their chest in non-traumatic circumstances, or via lifting the larynx to increase oesophageal lumen size.

An assessment of the placement of the orogastric or nasogastric tube should follow, including aspiration and gentle delivery of a syringe of air whilst auscultating over the stomach. Visualisation under laryngoscopy can also ensure there is no inadvertent tracheal placement.

Attach a drainage bag post insertion to facilitate hygienic drainage.

Nasogastric insertion of any tube is an acceptable alternative, except in facial trauma. Nasogastric tube sizing is the same as for an orogastric tube.

Take care to match the size of any suction catheter used with the airway, and ensure it slides in easily.

16.7 ONGOING MUSCLE RELAXATION - PANCURONIUM

Where drugs are provided to enable intubation, it should be anticipated that once they wear off, gagging and its consequent problems would return. In many instances it is preferable to provide for the long-term removal of these reflexes, to allow effective control of the airway and ventilation. Pancuronium is a drug with an effective duration of up to 45 minutes, and is suitable for this purpose.

16.7.1 INDICATIONS FOR ONGOING PARALYSIS

Though longer-term paralysis use will be common, it will not be always routinely used. The suggested settings for routine long-term paralysis use include:

- Patients with a primary neurological injury, which includes those with head trauma and those with a non-traumatic brain injury. These patients require protection from all means of rise in ICP including gagging. They also require careful control of ventilation and $ETCO_2$.
- Patients post cardiac arrest being managed with therapeutic cooling therapy. The paralysis is for the purpose of avoiding shivering that would be counter-productive to the cooling.
- For inter-hospital transfer use where paralysis has been deemed the best option for patient management.
- Any other setting where intubation is to be maintained, ventilation controlled, or sedation alone proves inadequate.

It is the latter setting that warrants most discussion. The use of sedation alone is the preferred method of maintaining most non-neurological ETTs in place. Signs that this is proving inadequate include:

- Return of gagging
- Forceful expiration attempting to displace the ETT
- Muscle activity such as back arching, biting or arm movements

Pancuronium is the longer-term paralysis agent selected for use in AV.

In such an event, Pancuronium will be needed to render the patient compliant with therapy. It should be noted that spontaneous breathing is not a specific indication for longer-term paralysis. Some patients can accommodate ETT placement without difficulty yet continue to breathe. Patients who are paralysed rely totally on positive pressure ventilation. This can have a detrimental impact on venous return and cardiac output due to the changed intrathoracic pressures. If it can be avoided at all, that is preferred.

Only draw up Pancuronium after ETT placement has been confirmed by capnography.

If required, administer Pancuronium as soon as the ETT is confirmed in place and secured. The initial Suxamethonium has a duration of 4 – 6 minutes. Be aware of the overlap period between the muscle relaxation of Suxamethonium and the onset time of the longer-term paralysis, i.e., Pancuronium has an onset of 2-3 minutes. It is important to avoid a period of non-paralysis that may produce unwanted gagging, patient distress and uncontrolled ventilation. Without adequate on-going paralysis (i.e., if Pancuronium administration is delayed too long) gagging may occur leading to a harmful ongoing rise in ICP.

Pancuronium has no sedative activity; it is only a muscle relaxant. As with Suxamethonium during the induction, adequate sedation must be maintained to avoid causing distress to the patient.

If muscle activity, movement or respiration is noted subsequent to initial administration, a repeat dose of Pancuronium may be administered. Be aware that the specific $ETCO_2$ waveform indicating spontaneous breathing is often a late sign of inadequate paralysis.

Patients, relatively non-disturbed, can be slow to show the diminished effects of paralysis wearing off. If the maximum 45 minutes is being approached and there are still no signs of muscle activity returning, administer the next dose of Pancuronium to avoid unwanted inadequate paralysis. This is particularly so when the patient is to be transferred to another hospital from the receiving emergency department.

If a patient is intubated without Suxamethonium (either no drug or sedation drugs only), Pancuronium can be administered, if it is required, after the correct ETT placement is confirmed by capnography.

Pancuronium is contraindicated to any patient who was demonstrating seizure activity prior to the initial intubation, even if Suxamethonium was used.

16.8 ONGOING SEDATION

Muscle relaxation does not affect the level of central nervous system awareness.

Sedation must be maintained concurrently with any paralysed patient. Sedation can be maintained with either 2.5 to 5mg Midazolam increments or a Morphine and Midazolam infusion. This should be commenced as soon as practical post intubation, once ETT placement is confirmed. The preferred method is for the first post ETT sedation to be a small bolus dose, with a follow up check of BP. This will allow for a guided determination of the ongoing sedation doses.

A Morphine and Midazolam infusion should be prepared by adding 30 mg of each drug to 30 ml of Normal Saline, and infused via syringe pump at a rate adequate to maintain an adequate level of sedation. This preparation will result in 1 mg of each drug in 1 ml of fluid. Commencing the infusion at 5 – 10 ml / hour will provide an appropriate starting point, and deliver 5 – 10 mg of each drug per hour.

Be aware of the hypotensive effects of the sedation drugs. Care will be required to balance the sedation needs and the blood pressure of the patient.

Where an increase in sedation is required by bolus, and a sedation infusion is running, the bolus must be given in increments of 2.5 – 5 ml of the drug mixture. This can be achieved by the 'purge' function on most syringe pumps. Simply increasing the infusion rate can take an excessive time frame to increase the required drug level due to the half life and therapeutic range of the drugs.

The patient should be continuously monitored for signs of inadequate sedation. This would be manifested by indications of a sympathetic response, including:

- Heart rate and blood pressure increasing together. Any sudden rise in these vital signs should prompt suspicion.
- Tearing / Lacrimation
- Diaphoresis

These signs may also indicate inadequate ventilation, hypoxia or displacement of the ETT. Always recheck ETT position and effective ventilation prior to increasing sedation.

If the patient shows signs of bite / cough / gag or is spontaneously breathing, increased paralysis is indicated. Whilst patient sedation must be maintained, aggressive use of sedation is not required. The role of sedation is to blunt patient awareness and to treat pain.

16.9 HYPOTENSION AND BLOOD PRESSURE MAINTENANCE

There are numerous threats to blood pressure during the intubation process. The drugs used in any drug-facilitated intubation can lead to vasodilatation and hypotension. Positive pressure ventilation increases intrathoracic pressure and reduces cardiac output. This will be particularly problematic with respiratory distressed patients. The presence of traumatic injuries can lead to bleeding and hypovolaemia.

Few patients benefit from hypotension, with head injuries being notably adversely affected. Vigilance must be maintained to monitor and manage blood pressure before, during, and after any intubation attempt.

Any hypotension should be managed aggressively as soon as practicable, using a fluid push of 20ml/kg isotonic crystalloid solution. This may be repeated if required. Attempt to maintain the blood pressure between 100 and 140 mmHg systolic. The clear preference is for a BP value of above 120 mmHg. Do not fluid fill if pulmonary oedema is suspected.

If hypotension continues despite adequate fluid replacement, consider an Adrenaline infusion at a starting rate of 5mcg per minute. Adrenaline is controversial in the setting of trauma and should not be used[6].

Reconsider any other potential causes of hypotension including tension pneumothorax or spinal injury.

Patients with non-traumatic causes of hypotension should have those issues addressed as appropriate. Cardiogenic, asthmatic, septic, allergic and drug induced causes may require clear assistance with inotrope, vasoactive or antiarrhythmic drugs, either in conjunction with or instead of volume replacement therapy. Manage as per guideline in each instance.

16.10 PATIENT WARMTH

Good normal patient management involves the maintenance of a normal body temperature. To assist with maintaining temperature control, minimise the exposure of the patient to cool air. It should be remembered that immobile patients, without muscle activity, lose body heat very quickly even in relatively warm environmental conditions.

Protection mechanisms include minimising exposure to cooler ambient air, removing damp clothing once in the protected ambulance cabin, closing vehicle doors promptly to remove draft/wind, keeping vehicle heaters running whilst out of the car, not using the air-conditioning, and generous use of blankets and temperature sheets.

Patients exposed to trauma suffer varying degrees of bleeding. Cooling can increase clotting times, increase haemorrhaging, and affect oxygen diffusion. Trauma patients should be kept normothermic.

Reactions to some illicit drugs and malignant hyperthermic responses to some medications can produce sudden hyperthermia. In either event, rapid cooling through external measures and cool intravenous fluids should follow to reduce the temperature below 38.5 degrees. Ongoing paralysis and sedation should be continued as normal. In the paralysed patient, look for sudden sharply rising $ETCO_2$ readings as much as relying on noting elevations in patient temperature and heart rate.

Therapeutic hypothermia post cardiac arrest has been shown to improve cerebral outcomes in these patients. As such, these patients should be cooled to recommended temperatures regardless of drug facilitated intubation performance. They are routinely longer term paralysed to remove muscular shivering.

16.11 CERVICAL COLLAR

Holding the head in a stable, non-moving neutral position is important in all intubation cases.

Placement of a cervical collar will reduce possible head movement reducing the potential for ETT displacement. Even normal flexion can allow the distal ETT end to come out of the trachea. Collar placement can be provided for all intubated patients, and should be applied for all drug assisted intubation patients.

Head trauma patients must receive good cervical care at all times. This applies during movements, transport and throughout the airway procedures. A cervical collar should be fitted early.

Any collar fitted prior to intubation must be released during the procedure to allow for jaw movement and mouth opening. An assistant can be delegated the task of monitoring and restricting head movements.

The collar needs to be pre-formed and properly fitted to ensure both effectiveness and to avoid causing jugular venous occlusion.

16.12 EYE CARE

Tape both patient eyes, to reduce mucosal drying in the absence of involuntary blinking.

16.13 PATIENT MOVEMENT AND TRANSFER

Patient movements are vulnerable times. There are a range of risks: ETT displacement, variation in delivery of ventilation, reduced supervision and attention paid to the patient, equipment repositioning and increased stimulation of the patient.

Before any movement of the patient, adequately plan, locate equipment and delegate tasks.

Ensure the airway paramedic holds the ETT and the patient's jaw with the same hand. A suggested technique is to pinch the ETT with the thumb and forefinger and hold the remaining fingers under the jaw.

The airway paramedic must co-ordinate, and controls all patient movements. Clear and loud instruction is required.

If using a bag/valve/mask, place it on the bed beside the patient's head, to avoid pulling on the ETT.

If using an Oxysaver™ or device that can pull on the ETT during movement, disconnect prior to any movement. If this is to occur, provide a number of ventilations quickly to ensure oxygenation prior to the disconnection.

As soon as practicable, reconnect the ETT and recommence ventilation.

Immediately recheck placement with $ETCO_2$, SpO_2, auscultation, and physiological parameters.

17 DRUG FACILITATED INTUBATION – WITHOUT PARALYSIS

The general principles of RSI apply in the IFS setting, and should be adhered to.

The respiratory distressed patient is distinct in that in the event of a failed intubation, the now paralysed patient will be very difficult to adequately ventilate. Underpinning any intubation performed with muscle relaxant drugs is the assumption that if the patient cannot be intubated, the risk is considerably less if the patient can continue spontaneous ventilation and not rely wholly on being supported.

It is important that prior to any intubation attempt, there is a period of support ventilation and pre-oxygenation period. This provides the reserve time and capacity to allow for an apnoeic period during the intubation attempt. Development of this reserve is less likely in the respiratory distressed patient, who will likely remain with poor blood gas chemistry throughout the procedure. Time will be imperative and the patient far less tolerant.

Many respiratory diseases have narrowing of the airways through bronchospasm, oedema fluid or foreign body obstruction. This leads to an increased level of resistance to air flow, demanding increased pressure in IPPV/APPV to open the smaller airways. This predisposes this group to:

- Being more difficult to ventilate
- Subsequent risks of barotrauma through excessive pressure in the fragile smallest airways
- Raising intrathoracic pressure, reducing venous return, cardiac output and blood pressure.

The patient in respiratory distress will be heavily reliant on their accessory muscles to increase ventilation. This is extremely tiring and leads to a very high oxygen demand from the respiratory muscles. It also results in greater CO_2 production and lactic acidosis.

17.1 HYPOXIC ILLNESS

Though hypoxia is a feature of all respiratory distress to some extent, in some situations it is the main factor. Hypoxia leads to anxiety and agitation prior to a loss of consciousness and eventual bradycardia and cardiovascular collapse. This group include the pulmonary oedema, aspiration and infective diseases. All these presentations have physical barriers to gas exchange and, in particular, delivery of oxygen to the pulmonary vasculature.

This group carries the greatest risk of intolerance to apnoeic periods having virtually no effective reserve of oxygen. Intubation attempts will have to be short with a return to bag/valve/mask immediately any difficulties are noted.

These patients can be managed in a semi upright posture even after loss of consciousness. Intubation can be performed in this position as long as the airway paramedic can gain suitable airway access.

- Postural gravity drainage will optimise effectiveness of the upper lung lobes.
- Once supine, fluid will flow from the trachea, making visualisation of the cords more difficult. In such instances, the airway paramedic may need to look for the source point of frothing or bubbling to visualise the opening to the trachea.
- Supine posturing will increase venous return. For the pulmonary oedema patient, this may increase myocardial workload and increase the fluid shifting into the alveoli.

Provide all supportive therapies to manage the underlying clinical condition. This includes drug therapies and non-invasive ventilation strategies such as Continuous Positive Airway Pressure (CPAP). Many of these patients can be improved to the point of not requiring intubation, and such options should be sought first.

Intubation should be a last resort for the respiratory failure patient. Having said that, once the patient is in respiratory failure, there must be no hesitation in taking over the role of airway and ventilation for such patients.

17.2 HYPERCAPNEIC ILLNESS

Diseases impacting on expiration result in retention of CO_2. Primarily the asthma / COPD group, these patients will have little reserve capacity of oxygen and will present as very difficult to ventilate.

The principle gas affecting patient presentation is increasing CO_2. Only at the end stage will oxygen levels fall away; when this deterioration occurs, there will be a quick deterioration to respiratory failure. Monitoring SpO_2 is important though it must be recognised this value may remain consistent until complete failure of respiration is imminent.

This group must be ventilated at less than usual minute volumes. The trapping of gas in the smallest airways will lead to hyperinflation and an increased intrathoracic pressure. The rate of ventilation during IPPV will be between 5 and 8 per minute and, on occasions even less. Hypercapneic patients with problems of gas trapping will be very sensitive to small changes in intrathoracic pressure.

- Where patients lose their pulse during ventilation, consideration must be given to the cause. In the asthma or COPD patient, if a good heart rhythm is present and IPPV is occurring, consider one-minute apnoea to reduce intrathoracic pressure. Application of gentle, lateral chest pressure, coinciding with any expiratory effort by the patient, will assist the expulsion of gas from the lungs. If pulse does not return, commence CPR, and administer inotropes and a crystalloid push to increase venous return.
- If a state of pulselessness continues, consider the presence of tension pneumothorax. This will be particularly applicable once the patient is intubated and the airway is sealed to leaks.

Though CO_2 will be the most problematic gas, manipulation of it will be difficult and even undesirable. Accepting the CO_2 value is very high and will remain so for some hours is important. This will be a gradual corrective process. More importantly, maintenance of SpO_2 is imperative as the patient will be less forgiving to deterioration here.

Provide all supportive therapies to manage the underlying clinical condition. This includes drug and IPPV strategies. The condition of many of these patients can be improved to the point where intubation is not required, and all such prior options should be sought. No patient should be intubated prior to at least one bolus of IV bronchodilator being administered. Any improvement in condition may affect the decision to intubate and will compound any ongoing ETT maintenance.

17.3 PULMONARY EMBOLUS

This is actually a problem of perfusion rather than ventilation. It may present as respiratory distress or a more varied presentation. The alveoli remain ventilated in this pathology whilst compromised blood delivery causes some alveoli to have less than an adequate blood flow to facilitate gas exchange.

It would not be uncommon for Pulmonary Embolus (PE) to go unrecognised at the time of event.

The severely affected patient will present with a degree of hypoxia and hypoxaemia. The affected alveoli will remain non-contributory with the remainder only able to provide a given quantity of oxygen attached to haemoglobin. As such, despite intubation, the oxygen saturation is likely to remain poor. The value of this treatment modality would have to be questioned.

In contrast, an adequate preload to the right heart will be required to maintain adequate perfusion through the lungs to the left heart. In the setting of a compromised perfusion state, anything worsening this predicament will likely lead to a dramatic cardiovascular compromise. If PE is suspected, significant attempts should be made to improve perfusion. The administration of sedation drugs is likely to dramatically affect blood pressure in the setting of PE.

17.4 DIABETIC KETOACIDOSIS

Patients in DKA requiring intubation do not have Suxamethonium administered. These patients are likely to have a high serum Potassium. This is a controversial contraindication as these patients are also likely to have low total and intracellular Potassium.

The DKA patient also has a significant metabolic acidosis. Once intubated, the ventilation of the patient will need to be specifically maintained so as to not compromise the respiratory alkalosis naturally occurring.

17.5   INTUBATION FACILITATED BY SEDATION – PRACTICAL ASPECTS

Though use of muscle relaxants is preferred in most intubation attempts, it is not preferred when intubating the respiratory failure patient.

The same sedative drugs as RSI are used and in the same doses. This will be Fentanyl 100mcg and Midazolam 0.1mg/kg. If the patient has a BP of < 100mmHg, a heart rate of >100, or an age > 60, use half sedation doses. These drugs are vasoactive and hypotension is to be avoided.

A pre-fluid load of crystalloid is desirable to offset the vasodilatation effects of the sedation drugs. This would, of course, not be desirable if pulmonary oedema is present or suspected.

There will be no fasciculation to observe. Look for relaxation of jaw tone after 30 – 45 seconds before commencing any intubation attempt. It is likely the relaxation will be short-lived, often as little as 15 – 30 seconds. Be prepared to intubate as soon as the jaw relaxation occurs. It is important not to rush or become over anxious at this stage, however expediency is necessary.

Airway resistance will already be increased. The largest possible ETT appropriate for the patient should be used to minimise adding to the airway resistance.

If **laryngoscopy is possible**, the cord view is grade one or two but intubation is still not possible due to jaw tone/gag factors, quickly administer one further dose of sedation equal to the first. This is an attempt to blunt residual gag on the assumption there simply was not enough sedation.

If **laryngoscopy is not possible** due to jaw tone continuing, administer one further dose of each sedation drug equal to the first in an attempt to blunt residual gag.

If **laryngoscopy is possible** but the cord view is grade three or four, no further sedation is to be administered. Sedation drugs do not change view, they change gag factors prohibiting a view. If the vocal cord view is consistent with a difficult intubation, further sedation offers little practical benefit but adds to the risk of the other actions of the drugs.

One of the disconcerting factors for the inexperienced practitioner using this intubation method is that the patient is not paralysed. As such, they may gag during laryngoscopy and they may continue to breathe throughout. It is the gag reflex that needs to be overcome. If the patient continues to breathe, more sedation is not indicated for that reason alone.

It is common to see movement of the vocal cords and they may not be fully apart, or they may be moving in and out with respiration. Attempt intubation whilst synchronising with the patient's respiratory pattern, i.e., intubate when the patient inhales to avoid undue vocal cord spasm or injury. The vocal cords may spasm during the intubation attempt if touched. If laryngeal spasm does occur, return to bag/valve/mask until airflow is restored and continue.

Where strong jaw tone and / or peripheral muscle tone are found, it is unlikely that this method alone will be successful in overcoming it. The airway paramedic needs to balance urgency and the need for intubation versus, likelihood of success. Intubating the respiratory distress patient requires a sense of timing and patience to wait for enough deterioration to allow intubation, but not to a point of cardiovascular or respiratory collapse.

A maximum of two doses of sedation are applicable.

The airway paramedic should wear eye safety and respiratory mask protection during any intubation attempt.

17.6 POST INTUBATION MANAGEMENT

The post intubation management of the respiratory distressed patient is very similar to any other drug-facilitated intubation. Placement confirmation checks are the same, as is the need for patient protection from the environment. Orogastric tube or nasogastric tube placement is important.

The non-paralysed patient may continue to breathe post intubation. This will affect the confirmation checks possible.

- A spontaneously breathing patient will be difficult to auscultate for placement. Air entry over the lung fields will be audible regardless of ETT placement. Abdominal gurgling would still suggest incorrect placement.
- $ETCO_2$ waveform will be the strongest confirmation of correct ETT placement.
- Anticipate a rise in SpO_2 when ETT placement is correct.

17.6.1 VENTILATION

Ongoing ventilation strategies for the respiratory distressed patient have been discussed earlier. Care is required with maintaining ventilation and $ETCO_2$ and SpO_2 figures, and the risks associated with APPV. The risk of barotrauma and raised intrathoracic pressure can be minimised with careful ventilation.

17.6.2 ONGOING SEDATION

Correct ventilation may bring about an improvement in patient condition. Whilst the initial induction sedation may be sufficient for the duration of ambulance management, it is more likely that further sedation will be required. Note that these drugs will have a longer duration of effect than the Suxamethonium used in RSI.

Sedation can be provided via bolus increments of Midazolam and Morphine or via an ongoing maintenance infusion. A Midazolam and Morphine infusion, as previously discussed, is the appropriate choice.

17.6.3 ONGOING PARALYSIS

Paralysis is not mandatory with all IFS patients. The indications to provide ongoing paralysis are gagging, or other patient responses, that suggest they are trying to reject the ETT from its placement. ICP rises are not as critical with this patient group, although it is desirable to avoid forceful rejection.

Sedation should be the first choice for ETT maintenance in this setting. Should gagging or ETT resistance be strong and forceful, or should more bolus increments be required within a several minute time period, the use of longer-term paralysis is indicated.

18

THE DIFFICULT INTUBATION

The majority of intubation attempts are described as having a clear vocal cord views. The paramedic should similarly experience this to be the case. However, the difficult or failed intubation attempt is a reality in any airway management arena. There will be numerous occasions for an IC paramedic, when a clear view on laryngoscopy cannot be achieved for a variety of patient and circumstantial reasons. An awareness of patient circumstances, and the inherent difficulties of their injury or condition, will enhance a paramedic's ability to successfully place an ETT. The defining characteristic of successfully dealing with intubation difficulties is an awareness of the fallback options, and an immediate response if they are required.

18.1   INITIAL INTUBATION

The initial intubation attempt should not be commenced until all preparation steps have been put into place for the equipment, the patient, and team coordination. Each actual attempt should not last more than 15 to 20 seconds. Should intubation not be possible at this point, a return to bag / valve / mask to maximise ventilation should follow immediately.

The major ramification of a difficult or failed intubation is an increased risk of airway compromise, and inadequate ventilation in the now paralysed and / or sedated patient. The continuous focus should become the provision of airway protection via suction, basic airway management and maintaining cricoid pressure.

There should be no more than two attempts at intubation on any one patient.

The most skilled practitioner should have made the first attempt. There should be no consideration for changing positions and roles. The second intubation attempt should follow soon after the first. This will be a point for consideration where IC instructors in training roles will need to balance patient interest with supervised junior practitioner attempts.

There should be no delay in moving onto the difficult / failed intubation process, as a satisfactory outcome must be achieved as soon as possible whilst the patient remains paralysed and / or sedated.

18.2   RE-OXYGENATION

A return to IPPV should follow immediately the first intubation attempt is unsuccessful.

Cricoid pressure needs to be maintained.

The duration of Suxamethonium is only a few minutes. The attempt to secure the airway is restricted in time. The re-oxygenation period should not take more than 30 to 60 seconds.

18.3 CORRECTIBLE FACTORS

If the vocal cord view has been obstructed, consider the following correcting actions:

- Suction foreign material / fluid
- Removal of foreign body, false teeth etc via Magill's forceps
- Use of laryngeal pressure and manual manipulation of the larynx
- Use of an alternate laryngoscope blade size
- Use of a smaller sized ETT
- Consider your laryngoscopy technique and positioning of the blade tip in the vallecular groove
- Adjust the patient head positioning. In non-trauma settings, consider slightly increasing the elevation of the head by ramping up until the external auditory meatus is on, or in advance of, a horizontal line to the lowest point of the suprasternal notch.

18.4 RE-ATTEMPTING INTUBATION

Once all possible corrections are instigated and the patient is adequately re-oxygenated, a second intubation should be attempted. This whole phase should be completed within 45–60 seconds.

Use of the bougie is mandatory on any second intubation attempt.

If the vocal cords cannot be brought immediately on view, attempt a blind intubation using the bougie.

If the patient is being intubated via the sedation only method due to a respiratory distress presentation, a second attempt should not occur if the glottic view was a grade 3 or 4 on first view.

If intubation is not possible after the second attempt, no further attempts should occur. Continue with the failed intubation drill.

18.5 SPECIFIC DIFFICULT INTUBATIONS

18.5.1 FACIAL AND AIRWAY BURNS

The patient with facial burns is both complex and dynamic. There are a range of issues that need to be considered surrounding facial and airway burns, as they all complicate any intubation attempt. This is the one group of patient who may need to be intubated early while the GCS is still adequate. Consultation with the receiving hospital is required if GCS is higher than indicated in the relevant guideline. Deterioration in conscious state may be associated with significant oedema and respiratory failure rendering an intubation attempt a great risk.

Oedema may be either present, or increase, during pre-hospital management. The concurrent administration of IV fluids is likely to worsen this situation. If intubation is considered likely, it should be before oedema becomes significant.

Oedema may make mouth opening difficult and reduce the external landmarks needed for cricothyroidotomy.

If facial burns are present, accompanying airway burns should be assumed. Upper airway protective mechanisms are quite successful at protecting the lower airways from short-term excesses in temperature, and will bear the initial brunt of damage. The signs of airway burns include facial burns, singed facial hair, cough, stridor, hoarse voice, and sputum containing carbon or soot.

Where lung damage is present, hypoxia is likely to follow. This will decrease the ability to tolerate inadequate ventilation and endure an apnoeic period during any intubation attempt.

Bronchospasm is common in this setting. The administration of nebulised bronchodilator therapy may compromise the ability to deliver an adequate amount of oxygen prior to intubation. The highest level of oxygen therapy able to provide suitable pre-oxygenation should be used, with the alternative of IV bronchodilators as required.

Pulse oximetry may be unreliable. It does not have the ability to properly distinguish from the carboxyhaemoglobin likely to be present post any smoke inhalation.

Suxamethonium is contraindicated in cases of high serum potassium. Burns older than 24 hours will show an increase in serum potassium; however this is not applicable in the early acute phase. RSI is the preferred option for intubation in the acute airway burn setting.

18.5.2 UPPER AIRWAY ANGIOEDEMA

Angioedema may present from a variety of causes including allergic response and as a side effect to some medications (most notably ACE inhibitors). Many of the upper airway issues described in facial burns apply here as well.

Medical angioedema will usually be treated with adrenaline if it presents with significant symptoms. Adrenaline may be administered by either the intramuscular or intravenous route, dependent on the patients' perfusion status. Give consideration to nebulised adrenaline to allow its direct delivery to the oedematous upper airways. This should not be allowed to compromise essential high concentration oxygen delivery.

Ideally allow an opportunity for such therapies to improve the patients' respiratory status, perfusion, and conscious state before proceeding with intubation.

18.5.3 FACIAL TRAUMA

If a significant derangement to the facial / jaw / airway structures is present, consider your ability to be able to place an ETT. Insufficient middle to lower facial structures may inhibit the ability to adequately apply laryngoscopy, or to identify the location of the glottic opening or oesophagus.

The airway assessment should include an assessment of the amount of blood or fluid in the airway, and if suction will be adequate to clear the airway. Lateral positioning and gravitational drainage may assist.

If either of the preceding issues are factors, do not proceed with an RSI.

If it is appropriate to continue with the intubation attempt, be prepared for the initially clear view to disappear quickly. Blood may cover the laryngoscope blade, leading to a 'red' view very quickly.

Ensuring the backup laryngoscope and blade are in working order during the preparation phase is essential.

THE FAILED INTUBATION

Despite all attempts at corrective actions and bougie use, the second attempt at intubation may still not see successful tracheal placement. The second intubation attempt is the first step in the failed intubation drill. If that proves unsuccessful, continue following the flow chart of the failed intubation drill.

The intention of the failed intubation drill is to secure the airway and ventilation until muscle relaxants wear off and spontaneous ventilation returns. The intention is to put in place the best airway security, secondary to ETT placement.

As soon as the second attempt is unsuccessful, insert either an oropharyngeal or a nasopharyngeal airway and return to bag / valve / mask ventilation. Continue until the patient recovers spontaneous ventilation.

When the patient recovers spontaneous ventilation, they should be placed in a lateral position with due consideration to other injuries.

19.1 LARYNGEAL MASK AIRWAY

In the event of being unable to ventilate the patient effectively via bag / valve / mask, the immediate fallback position is the placement of an LMA. As with all other elements of the failed intubation drill, an LMA insertion should be expeditious.

The LMA is placed blindly into the lower pharynx over the glottis. It is easier and quicker to place than an ETT. It can also be placed without neck flexion making it suitable for spinal trauma.

There is a decreased risk of aspiration with the LMA. However, it should not be considered as a substitute for intubation. It does provide some protection from the risk of blood aspiration in trauma.

The LMA can provide as good a tidal volume as a bag/valve/mask. It provides a low–pressure seal decreasing the risk of intragastric pressure forcing regurgitation. This is problematic though when there is increased lung compliance as in pulmonary oedema, pulmonary fibrosis, morbid obesity and asthma. In these cases, it can be difficult to ventilate effectively.

Once positioned and secured, the paramedic can continue to provide ventilation with only one hand.

Consider the likelihood of restlessness, irritability, trismus etc returning if these factors existed prior to paralysis. The correction of any hypoxia may alleviate some of these factors. The LMA requires an absent gag reflex to allow insertion. As soon as a gag reflex returns, the LMA will need to be removed. Sedation is not to be used to maintain the LMA in-situ.

The LMA should be inserted in the head neutral position. No change to head positioning should be required. Insert as per normal Clinical Work Instructions (CWI). If there is an inability to gain an adequate seal once positioned, consider changing the LMA for a smaller size down. The cuff of the LMA is trying to contact a relatively large airway area under low pressure to gain the seal. If it is unable, reducing the size of the area requiring contact can improve the chance of an effective seal.

Once inserted, the LMA cannot be moved off centre as an ETT can. In this setting, the lower part of the LMA would no longer be properly seated and would not be effective. Do not omit an appropriate soft bite block as trismus may return post paralysis. Two soft bite blocks may assist with maintaining the central position. Securing should be via a quick release knot, or proprietary device, that will permit a rapid removal if the patient recovers there gag reflex or conscious state.

Indicative $ETCO_2$ monitoring can be connected in line with the LMA.

The insertion (or removal) of an LMA is less likely to cause a cardiovascular response than an ETT. If removal is needed, then LMAs are to be withdrawn fully inflated to sweep the airway of accumulated secretions.

19.2   CRICOTHYROIDOTOMY

In the event of a complete inability to satisfactorily secure the airway and provide a level of ventilation post a failed intubation, cricothyroidotomy is the final act to secure that aim. It will have been preceded by all genuine attempts to ventilate via bag/valve/mask, nasopharyngeal or oropharyngeal airway and LMA.

It needs to be performed expeditiously, ideally before the Suxamethonium wears off and airway movement returns. It should be performed as per appropriate work instructions using a clean rather than a sterile technique.

Before commencement of the procedure, the cricothyroid landmark needs to be identified and marked. This should be performed routinely in the original set up for intubation. Draw a line in pen across the cricoid membrane.

All kit contents need to be laid out prior to any attempt at insertion. This should be on a clean, flat surface such as a towel or pillowcase. The kit does not require to be opened during the intubation set up.

Position the patient in a head neutral position with further head re-positioning unlikely to be necessary.

Don't discard the sharps, including the scalpel or introducing needle, too early as they may need to be used again. Place them into the now empty kit container. Take deliberate care with the placement and ultimate disposable of the now used and contaminated sharps.

Placement in the trachea is confirmed by the sudden loss of resistance as the trachea is penetrated followed by the ability to freely aspirate air via a syringe. As with the ETT, secure the cricothyroid catheter as soon as possible.

Once the needle is secured in place, ventilation is via the 'jet' technique. Quick and regular forceful puffs with generous tidal volume are applied to the normal bag / circuit at a rate of 30 per minute.

Capnography is not applicable during jet ventilation. The cricothyroidotomy needle is too narrow and ventilation too rapid for exhalation to flow backward into the needle. As a consequence pulse oximetry will increase in importance.

This procedure is a high risk – low frequency of performance skill. It **must** be practised regularly to maintain proficiency.

If the cricothyroidotomy becomes dislodged, recommence the insertion procedure from the start – except for the scalpel incision.

20 ADVERSE OUTCOMES

Except in a failed intubation, the unfavourable outcomes that are possible following an intubation attempt include procedural injury, an incorrect ETT placement or unwanted drug effects.

20.1 PROCEDURAL INJURY

Injury can be sustained through poor technique or through lack of attention to detail in management of the patient. Possible injuries include:

- Damaged and broken teeth from pressure applied by the laryngoscope blade due to poor technique.
- Trauma to the larynx from contact with the ETT during insertion. This is particularly so if insertion is forced or without due care.
- Spinal damage in trauma patients whose neck is manipulated during intubation. This is also possible in the elderly patient who has cervical malformation or degeneration.
- Any patient not adequately paralysed and muscle relaxed can bite on the ETT causing a period of hypoxia. A suitable 'bite block' should be inserted post intubation and drug therapy supplied post intubation as required.
- Unrecognised obstruction of the ETT with blood, secretions, or mucous.

20.2 INCORRECT ETT PLACEMENT

There are two likely stages in which an ETT may be incorrectly placed. The first is at the time of insertion. The second is if it becomes displaced during patient management.

An ETT incorrectly placed is not a problem in itself. From time to time all paramedics will incorrectly place an ETT. The real problem is when the incorrect placement goes unrecognised. Either a fatal outcome or significant brain damage would be likely.

No intubation attempt should be commenced without waveform capnography being available. Placement of the ETT should be confirmed as soon as possible. Where any doubt exists, the ETT should be removed and an immediate return to bag/valve/mask should follow.

Visualisation of the ETT passing between cords is unreliable. Sight can be lost, particularly if the view is a difficult one.

The correct position for the ETT is so that the cuff is only just past the vocal cords. As such, any flexion of the neck causes the ETT to move up and down in the trachea. Once an ETT moves out (even if the cuff is inflated), it is unlikely that further head movement will correctly reposition the tube back in the trachea. Even relatively small head or neck movements may lead to ETT dislodgement. Diligent clinical observation and checking of the ETT position is required.

An ETT inserted too deeply will be positioned in a main bronchus, usually the right. Insertion depth should be checked immediately upon placement then rechecked regularly. The ETT should be secured at that depth and a note of such depth made on patient handover. Auscultation should be performed to compare lung air entry, as capnography may not provide clues as to bronchial placement. The black line on the distal end of the ETT should be positioned just through the vocal cords, to avoid an excessively deep placement.

The ODD can indicate bronchial placement. Instead of the free pull back on the plunger, effective withdrawal is possible with the plunger pulling back in a short distance when released.

During any patient movement, the ETT should be thoroughly rechecked to ascertain correct position. The ETT should be securely fastened as soon as practicable. The airway paramedic should retain control and supervision of the ETT and all patient movements at all times.

An unrecognised placement of the ETT into the oesophagus is a disastrous occurrence, and will result in either a very poor outcome or the death of the patient.

20.3 UNWANTED DRUG EFFECTS

Hypotension is the dominant side effect of the sedation drugs used in the procedure.

Vasodilation is a potential side effect of the sedation drugs, particularly Midazolam. Subsequent hypotension can lead to a compromised cerebral perfusion, since Mean Arterial Pressure (MAP) must override intracranial pressure (MAP − ICP = CPP). The ICP will be rising in the setting of head trauma and neurological injury. Maintenance of adequate blood pressure is imperative.

Systolic blood pressure needs to be maintained between 100 and 140mmHg. This may require considerable fluid/volume expansion via crystalloid infusion. **A distinct preference is for blood pressure to be at least 120mmHg systolic, in terms of guideline.**

The use of adrenaline in the setting of head trauma is not consistent with good patient outcomes.

20.3

21 / RAPID SEQUENCE INTUBATION – TIMELINES

The following is a suggested overview of relevant time frames for the steps involved in pre-hospital Rapid Sequence Intubation, and is based upon a similar concept utilised by the Royal Australian College of Anaesthetists.

RAPID SEQUENCE INTUBATION
TIME LINE A

MINUS **5 min**	**Pre-oxygenate with 100 % oxygen** **Prepare advanced airway equipment** **Record vital signs**
TIME ZERO	**Administer Sedation and Paralysing Agents** • Light Cricoid Pressure • Fentanyl 100 mcg (50 mcg) IVI • Midazolam 0.1 mg / Kg (0.05 mg / Kg or 1 mg) IVI • Suxamethonium 1.5 mg / Kg IVI • Firm Cricoid Pressure
30 sec **45 sec**	**Observe fasciculation / signs of paralysis** **Endotracheal Intubation**

75 sec	**Intubation Achieved**
	• Check and confirm correct placement
	   – ODD
	   – Inflate cuff
	   – $ETCO_2$
	   – Tracheal Squash Test
	   – Auscultate Chest
	• If not confirmed, immediate Difficult / Failed RSI Drill (Refer to Time Line B)
	• Bite Block
	• Recommence ventilation
	• Secure
	• Remove Cricoid Pressure

2 – 4 min **PLUS**	**Long Term Paralysis** • Pancuronium 8mg IVI • Orogastric Tube • ETT Suction • Tape eyes • Additional sedation / infusion
	• Atropine may be administered at any time if indicated • Correct hypotension at any time as per relevant guidelines • Manage other injuries on a priority and needs basis i.e., chest injuries, musculo-skeletal trauma

DIFFICULT / FAILED INTUBATION DRILL
TIME LINE B

TIME ZERO **75 sec**	**Difficult / Failed Intubation Drill** • Immediate Difficult / Failed RSI Drill • Re-oxygenate with manual ventilation
2 min	**Re-Attempt Intubation** • Bougie • Smaller size ETT • Identify and manage other corrective factors
2 min 30 sec	**Intubation Achieved** • Check and confirm correct placement as per RSI Time Line A
3 min	**If ETT Placement not confirmed – Failed Intubation Drill** • Remove ETT • Re-oxygenate with manual ventilation • If unable to ventilate with OP airway in-situ proceed to LMA
3 min 30 sec	**Laryngeal Mask Airway** • Insert LMA • Check and confirm correct placement • If incorrect placement or unable to ventilate with LMA • Remove LMA • Re-oxygenate with manual ventilation • Proceed to Cricothyroidotomy
4 min 30 sec **PLUS**	**Cricothyroidotomy** • Insert Cricothyroidotomy • Ventilate patient • Secure

Pulse oximetry provides a continuous non-invasive measurement of arterial oxygen saturation (SpO_2). The monitoring of SpO_2 can provide an early warning of hypoxaemia, before clinical signs reflect the change. Pro-active treatment before profound hypoxaemia develops can then be initiated. SpO_2 represents one half of the ventilation equation and should be used in conjunction with $ETCO_2$ monitoring.

Pulse oximetry works by calculating the ratio of oxygenated haemoglobin to all the haemoglobins detected. The sensor probe has two rapidly alternating lights, red and infrared; this corresponds to the wavelengths of the two haemoglobins. The technology works out the difference between each separate light and displays the results as a percentage.

Oxyhaemoglobin Dissociation Curve

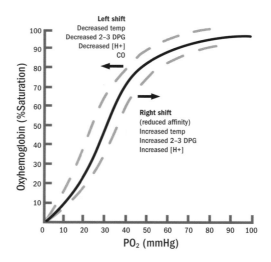

Source; Anaesthesia UK – ww.frca.co.uk - May 2009

The correlation between SpO_2 and PaO_2 is graphed via the Oxyhaemoglobin Dissociation Curve. The standard curve assumes a normal, healthy patient with standard values of pH, CO_2 and temperature.

Initially there is only a small effect as the PaO_2 decreases from 100%, however the curve steepens as SpO_2 levels reduce. For patient care purposes, a significant change in steepness occurs at a SpO_2 level of ~90%.

PaO_2 – mmHg	SpO_2 – %	Comments
100	100	
90	97	99 – 96% is normal for most people, (92 – 93% is the lower limit in some patients).
80	94	
70	92	90 – 85% — mild tissue hypoxia — regional or global.
60	89	
50	84	85 – 75% — significant widespread tissue hypoxia.
40	75	
30	57	< 75% severe hypoxia — cardiac arrest threatened.

Various factors can 'move' the curve, with resultant effects on oxygen availability to tissues.

Left Shift: A shift to the left implies an increased affinity between Hb and oxygen, with decreased oxygen transfer at the tissue level. Alkalosis, hypocapnia and a reduction in temperature cause a shift to the left.

Right Shift: Conversely, a shift to the right indicates lesser affinity, easier dissociation at the tissue level and increased oxygen availability to distal tissue. This also implies increased difficulty of oxygen attachment at the alveolar level. A right shift is associated with an increased acidic environment.

Pulse oximetry has many limitations that all need to be understood and appreciated to allow for its effective use as a monitoring adjunct;

- It only reflects the supply of oxygen. It does not reflect adequacy of ventilation and does not discuss removal of CO_2. This is particularly important with the CO_2 retainer, such as the asthmatic and the COPD patient. This patient can have failing respiration with even a loss of consciousness regardless of acceptable oxygen saturation.
- It is dependent on detection of peripheral pulses. States of poor perfusion and cardiac output cause a loss of accuracy. Pulse oximetry is inaccurate in shocked states, hypothermia and in chronic smokers.

Probes are designed for finger placement, and this will provide the most accurate result. Toes and ear lobes can be used. These alternatives are particularly useful in paediatric settings. Whatever the choice, a long lead to keep the monitor in paramedic view needs to be available. The rate of desaturation increases below 93%. It is highly preferable for intubation attempts and absences in oxygenation to occur with readings above this figure. The higher the initial oxygen saturation reading, the longer the period available before desaturation occurs.

Numerous factors may affect SpO_2 readings:

> POOR SIGNAL DETECTION
> - Poor probe position (including long fingernails)
> - Motion
> - Cold / vasoconstriction
> - Inflated blood pressure cuffs will reduce pulse strength
> - A too tight probe squeezed onto a finger/ear lobe or cheek
> - Cosmetic, ceramic, black finger nails

➤ FALSELY LOW SpO$_2$
  - Dark skin pigmentation
  - Dyes can interfere with light absorption – either dyes within the blood (such as those injected during cardiac procedures) or external dyes such as nail polish or dirty fingers
  - Infrared heating lamps

➤ FALSELY HIGH SpO$_2$
  - Oxygen bound with carboxyhaemoglobin in carbon monoxide poisoning can provide a reasonable SpO$_2$ reading exaggerating the amount of oxygen actually available. Methaemoglobin will provide similar observation
  - Intense fluorescent lights. If the ambient lighting is very bright, the probe can be covered with a cloth or blanket.

23

END TIDAL CO$_2$ MONITORING

End Tidal CO$_2$ (ETCO$_2$) measurement is the accepted 'gold standard' for affirming endotracheal tube placement.

ETCO$_2$ measures the partial pressure of carbon dioxide (CO$_2$) at the end of the expiration–ventilation cycle. ETCO$_2$ is a reflection of arterial CO$_2$ partial pressure (PaCO$_2$), which is in turn a reflection of cardiac output

Two methods of gas sampling are available, 'Mainstream' and 'Sidestream'.

- The Mainstream method has the infrared scanning 'in-line' at a direct point in the ventilation circuit, usually adjacent to the endotracheal tube. Mainstream utilises an in-line scanning device, which is potentially prone to damage and can be expensive.
- The Sidestream method draws a minute gas sample from the ventilation circuit, which is transported to the main unit for scanning via small diameter tubing. The Sidestream method is potentially subject to obstruction of the sample tubing by airway excretion or excess moisture. It may take longer than six ventilations in a Sidestream system to register a waveform on the capnograph.

A normally ventilating, haemodynamically stable patient has a specific identifiable waveform that reflects the CO$_2$ values at various phases of ventilation. Variations to normal ventilatory patterns can be discerned from identifiable abnormal waveforms. Any mechanical or physiological factor affecting CO$_2$ pulmonary diffusion will affect the ETCO$_2$ value.

Although there is no direct correlation between ETCO$_2$ and PaCO$_2$, in a healthy volunteer of normal weight, it is accepted the PaCO$_2$ will be ~3 to 5 mmHg higher. However, in compromised or sedated patients the variation may be up far more significant.

Other potential pre-hospital uses could include;

- Adjustment of ventilation parameters in the head injured trauma patient
- Apnoea detection in the spontaneously ventilating patient
- Endotracheal tube dislodgement
- An early indication of a reduced pulmonary perfusion, and
- Efficiency of CPR

23.1   END TIDAL CO$_2$ WAVE FORMS

On an ETCO$_2$ capnograph specific waveform patterns are recognisable, some examples of which are below. It is important to be able to recognise and understand the normal and abnormal waveform patterns. The potential causes and corrective actions required for abnormal patterns should also be understood.

WAVEFORM EXAMPLES

> **A** – NORMAL WAVEFORM

- A – B Baseline
- B – C Expiratory Upstroke
- C – D Expiratory Plateau
- D – ETCO$_2$ value
- D – E Inspiration Begins

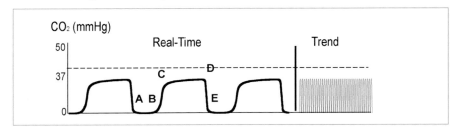

> **B** – ETT IN THE OESOPHAGUS

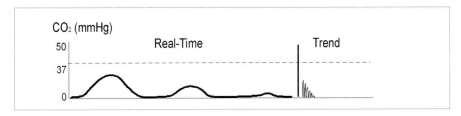

- Possible Causes:
  - ETT incorrectly placed in oesophagus
  - Patient has lost cardiac output
- Corrective Actions:
  - Confirm presence or absence of pulse
  - Remove ETT and return to APPV with Bag/Valve/Mask
  - Difficult / Failed Intubation Drill

➤ C – INADEQUATE ETT SEAL

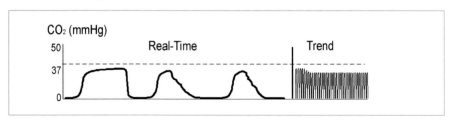

- Possible Causes:
    - Leaky or deflated ETT or tracheotomy cuff
    - Artificial airway too small for patient
    - Cuff herniation through the vocal cords
- Corrective Actions:
    - Check inflation pressure of ETT cuff
    - Consider a larger diameter ETT
    - Check the length at lips. The ETT may have moved upwards, particularly if cuff 'top ups' have been required.

➤ D – INCREASING ETCO$_2$

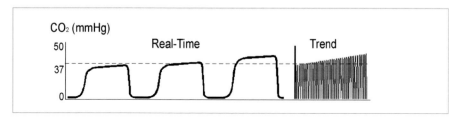

- Possible Causes:
    - Decrease in respiratory rate
    - Decrease in tidal volume
    - Increase in metabolic rate
    - Rapid rise in body temperature (hyperthermia)
- Corrective Actions:
    - Adjust ventilation parameters
    - Consider a potential cause of hyperthermia and manage if possible

> ➤ E – DECREASING ETCO$_2$

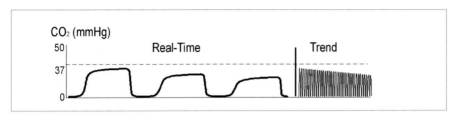

- Possible Causes:
  - Increase in respiratory rate
  - Increase in tidal volume
  - Decrease in metabolic rate
  - Fall in body temperature
  - Tension pneumothorax
- Corrective Actions:
  - Adjust ventilation parameters
  - Exclude tension pneumothorax
  - Consider possible cause of hypothermia and manage if possible

> ➤ F – REBREATHING

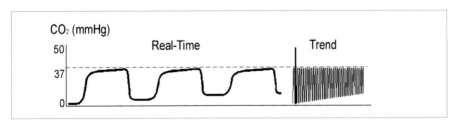

- Possible Causes:
  - Faulty inspiratory or expiratory valve
  - Inadequate inspiratory flow
  - Malfunction of CO$_2$ absorber
- Corrective Actions:
  - Adjust ventilation parameters
  - Switch to non-rebreathing resuscitator with high flow oxygen supply

> G – BREATHING CIRCUIT OBSTRUCTION

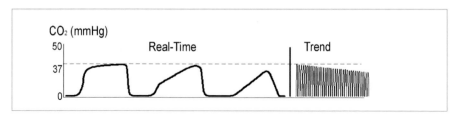

- Possible Causes:
  - Partially kinked or occluded artificial airway
  - Foreign body in the airway
  - Obstruction in expiratory limb of circuit
  - Bronchospasm
- Corrective Actions:
  - Suction ETT
  - Switch to non-rebreathing resuscitator with high flow oxygen supply
  - Manage bronchospasm

> H – INADEQUATE MUSCLE RELAXATION (CURARE CLEFT)

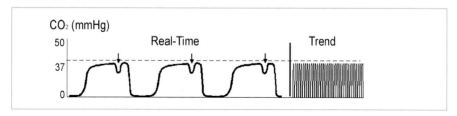

- Possible Causes:
  - Muscle relaxant subsiding
  - Depth of cleft inversely proportional to degree of drug activity
- Corrective Actions:
  - Increase paralysis

> I – FAULTY VENTILATOR CIRCUIT VALVE

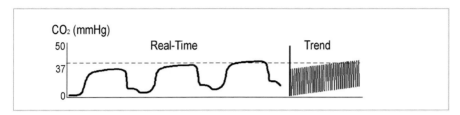

- Possible Causes:
  - Elevated baseline and abnormal descending limb of capnogram indicates the patient is rebreathing exhaled gas
- Corrective Actions:
  - Switch to a non–rebreathing resuscitator with high flow oxygen supply

24 END TIDAL CO₂ AND PULSE OXIMETRY DEVICES

Ambulance Victoria use two devices for measuring $ETCO_2$ and Pulse Oximetry; the Novametrix Tidal Wave Sp Monitor™, and the Phillips Heartstart MRx™ cardiac monitor.

The Novametrix Tidal Wave Sp Monitor™ is a Mainstream model, whilst the Phillips Heartstart MRx™ uses the Sidestream method. AV paramedics are referred to the operating manuals for each device for their specific instructions.

It is essential to be familiar with all controls, alarm functions and available screen or viewing options of any monitoring equipment. It is also necessary to be aware of how to quickly change any battery or alternate power source. The ability to problem solve a capnograph or pulse oximetry quandary will directly impact on the paramedics' ability to either accurately assess, or to intubate, the patient.

It is imperative all attachments directly involved in $ETCO_2$ monitoring are clean, and free from contamination, secretions and blood. Take care with the handling of any Mainstream device connector or adaptor, as 'window' cleanliness is essential to an accurate reading. Take care to not cut or damage the main cable of a Mainstream unit, and recognise the distal sensing apparatus is potentially fragile.

It may be possible to check the workings of the capnograph before use by gently blowing through the sensor and assessing the numerical and graphical information.

Ensure all connections, attachments, and tubing are firmly in place.

In general terms, the following are recommended settings for general use, accurate viewing and alarm settings of either these two devices, or for $ETCO_2$ / SpO_2 monitoring generally.

- Have all waveforms filled in or 'solid' if possible
- Ensure mmHg as the $ETCO_2$ units
- If available, use the gas compensation setting of 60% oxygen
- Have alarm or alerts enabled, and have the settings to high or very loud
- Use a longer $ETCO_2$ or SpO_2 averaging time option if possible
- Disable any auto power off or power / screen saving feature
- Use the extreme value alarms settings of;
  - $ETCO_2$ – High 80 & Low 10 mmHg
  - Respiratory Rate – High 30 & Low 8 / minute
  - SpO_2 – High 100 & Low 90%
  - Heart Rate – High 150 & Low 50 / minute
- If various screens are available, ensure the $ETCO_2$ capnograph screen is visible

25 ADDITIONAL DRUG INFORMATION

This section provides additional information on the paralysis agents, Suxamethonium and Pancuronium. Ambulance Victoria has selected these two agents as the primary drugs for pre-hospital use in their environment. These two drugs have been contextually discussed earlier in this text; the following information is provided as an adjunct to those previous discussions, and deals with some aspects specifically of interest to Ambulance Victoria.

25.1 SUXAMETHONIUM CHLORIDE

GENERAL INFORMATION

Suxamethonium is a short acting neuromuscular blocking agent, which is also known as Succinylcholine, Scoline or Anectine.

It can increase intragastric pressure by up to 85 cm H20. This means there is an increased risk of gastric expulsion leading to and during fasciculation, which may lead to an increased risk of aspiration. APPV should be ceased immediately after the administration of Suxamethonium to avoid further increasing gastric pressure by the inadvertent entry of oxygen / air into the alimentary tract.

CONTRAINDICATIONS

Upper airway obstruction: There will be an increased risk of failed intubation and fewer fall back options available.

Severe respiratory distress: There will be an increased risk of failed intubation and increased difficulty in managing the paralysed, non-intubated patient.

Penetrating eye injury: The drug can increase intraocular pressure leading to further eye damage and content expulsion.

High serum potassium: Diseases or injuries, including renal failure, significant and prolonged crush syndrome, and/or burns after 24 hours, cause higher serum potassium. During the fasciculation process there is a further potassium release. A patient found lying immobile with pressure areas to limbs for an extended period should be considered to have elevated potassium.

Organophosphate poisoning: Organophosphates produce an acetylcholine like action similar to Suxamethonium. The risk of excessive and prolonged neuromuscular blockade follows.

Ruptured abdominal aortic aneurysm: There is a decrease in intra-abdominal pressure post fasciculation due to skeletal muscle relaxation. The decreased intra-abdominal pressure can lead to decreased aortic tamponade and a subsequent increase in haemorrhage that may be catastrophic.

Known history of Suxamethonium apnoea: This is unlikely to be known in the field. Rarely, there may be a very long neuromuscular blockade period (a number of hours) after administration.

Malignant hyperthermia: This is rare; however the drug can produce a sudden and dramatic rise in metabolic rate and subsequent body temperature. Onset is usually within 30 minutes, if not more rapidly, and may be difficult to detect. Recognition may be through a noticeable rise in $ETCO_2$ not correctable with increased ventilation, a drop in SpO_2 due to increased oxygen uptake, unusually hot soda–lime in the Oxysaver™ canister, or through a detectable increase in body temperature. Malignant hyperthermia should be considered as life threatening as heat stroke. If recognised, manage as for heat stroke and notify the receiving hospital. The hospital treatment includes the use of Dantrolene as an antidote.

PRECAUTIONS

Liver disease, elderly patients and crush injuries all involve either conditions or associated medications that may lead to elevated serum potassium.

Non-fasted patients: There is a risk of regurgitation and aspiration of gastric contents. Most pre–hospital patients will have this as a risk factor.

Crush Injuries: The risk of an increase in serum potassium is high, as explained in the previous section.

Airway trauma: There will be an increased difficulty intubating the airway with greater risk of failed intubation.

Excessive acetylcholine effects leading to a bradycardia should be immediately managed with an 0.6mg increment of Atropine.

Suxamethonium requires refrigeration. In colder months weekly rotation of the drug is required. During the hotter months the more frequent rotation of every second day is needed. Longevity of the drug is prolonged by storage in cool fluid packs where available.

If more than one ampoule of drug is required, draw the second ampoule up in a separate syringe, with the ampoule attached. This is to avoid inadvertent over administration.

A second dose of Suxamethonium is likely to produce profound, unwanted effects including bradycardia, possibly asystole, prolonged duration, tachycardia and hyperkalaemia. **Do not administer a second dose.**

25.2 PANCURONIUM BROMIDE

Once the ETT is correctly placed, there may be an ongoing need to maintain paralysis to allow for continued placement. A longer acting muscle relaxant facilitates this. Pancuronium is such a drug.

GENERAL INFORMATION

Pancuronium is a non–depolarising, neuromuscular blocking agent. This will provide longer-term paralysis.

It does not cause any fasciculation, as it is a large molecule that does not enter or stimulate receptor sites.

It has longer duration of action (35–45 minutes).

It must only be administered post confirmation of tracheal intubation to avoid the risk of longer-term paralysis in the field intubation setting. Do not draw up Pancuronium until the ETT position is confirmed by capnography.

CONTRAINDICATIONS

Pancuronium administration must be accompanied by continual monitoring of vital signs, $ETCO_2$ and SpO_2. If these are not available the drug should not be used, since ETT displacement and / or difficulties with ventilation may not be otherwise detected.

The status epilepticus patient should not receive Pancuronium, except with direct medical instruction. Ongoing/continuous seizure activity will not be observed and may go undetected, and therefore not be managed correctly.

PRECAUTIONS

Adequate sedation always needs to be administered prior to, and accompanying, any paralysing agent to ensure a lack of patient awareness.

Pancuronium is metabolised via hepatic pathways onto at least three metabolites with less potency. About 80% of the drug and its metabolites are excreted in urine. The remaining 10% is excreted unchanged in faeces, with a small amount excreted in the bile.

Pancuronium is known to have an extended period of activity in elderly patients.

Pancuronium is drawn up into a 5ml syringe to provide for standardisation and to minimise drug errors. The initial dose is usually 8mg.

Pancuronium also requires refrigeration. Similar to Suxamethonium, in colder month's weekly rotation of drug is required. During the hotter months the more frequent rotation of every second day is needed. Longevity of the drug is prolonged by storage in cool fluid packs where available.

GLOSSARY

BP	Blood Pressure
cm	centimetre
CO$_2$	Carbon Dioxide
COPD	Chronic Obstructive Pulmonary Disease
CPAP	Continuous Positive Airway Pressure
CPP	Cerebral Perfusion Pressure
CPR	Cardiopulmonary Resuscitation
ED	Emergency Department
ETCO$_2$	End Tidal Carbon Dioxide
ETT	Endotracheal Tube
FG	French Gauge – sizing guide to nasogastric or orogastric tubes
GCS	Glasgow Coma Score
H$_2$O	Water
ICP	Intracranial Pressure
ISO	International Standards Organisation
IV	Intravenous
IFS	Intubation Facilitated by Sedation
kg	kilogram
LMA	Laryngeal Mask Airway
lpm	litres per minute
MAP	Mean Arterial Pressure
ml	millilitre
NPA	Nasopharyngeal Airway

ODD Oesophageal Detector Device (Wee Tester)

OPA Oropharyngeal Airway

O₂ Oxygen

PCO₂ Partial pressure of Carbon Dioxide

PEEP Positive End Expiratory Pressure

RSA Respiratory Status Assessment

RSI Rapid Sequence Intubation

SpO₂ Arterial O_2 saturation, expressed as a percentage

TBI Traumatic Brain Injury

The following articles are provided to provide a reference point for paramedics to the recent history and additional international experiences of pre-hospital intubation and RSI.

Bernard, S., et al. (2002). The use of rapid sequence intubation by ambulance paramedics for patients with severe head injury. *Emergency Medicine*, 14. 406–411

Davis, D.P., et al. (2003). The effect of paramedic rapid sequence intubation on outcome in patients with severe traumatic brain injury. Journal of Trauma, *Infection & Critical Care*, 54. 444-453.

Evans, T., & Carroll, P. (2001). Rapid sequence intubation; There are ways of identifying impending respiratory failure. American Journal of Nursing, 101 Supplement. 16-20.

Emergency Medicine (2002) 14, 406–411

ORIGINAL RESEARCH

The use of rapid sequence intubation by ambulance paramedics for patients with severe head injury

Stephen Bernard,[1,2] Karen Smith,[2] Shane Foster,[1] Phillip Hogan[1] and Ian Patrick[1]

[1]Air Ambulance Victoria and [2]Department of Epidemiology and Preventive Medicine, Monash University, Melbourne, Victoria, Australia

Abstract

Objective: To determine the effects of rapid sequence intubation in patients with severe head injury performed by paramedics on a helicopter emergency medical service.

Methods: The patient care records for patients with severe head injury who underwent rapid sequence intubation between November 1999 and February 2002 (inclusive) were examined. Data were extracted on the demographics of the patients, as well as the physiological changes before and after rapid sequence intubation.

Results: There were 122 patients with severe head injury evaluated at the scene during the study period. Rapid sequence intubation was attempted in 110 patients and was successful in 107 (97%). Intubation was associated with improvements in systolic blood pressure, oxygen saturation and end-tidal carbon dioxide levels, compared with baseline levels.

Conclusion: Rapid sequence intubation in patients with severe head injury may be safely undertaken by helicopter-based ambulance paramedics and is associated with improvements in oxygenation, ventilation and blood pressure. Further studies of this skill undertaken by road-based paramedics are warranted.

Key words: *endotracheal intubation, prehospital, severe head injury, suxamethonium.*

Introduction

Following severe head injury, many patients have decreased oxygenation and ventilation and this may cause a secondary brain injury.[1] In addition, a depressed gag and/or cough reflex may lead to aspiration of vomit and the subsequent pneumonitis may be fatal or result in a prolonged stay in an ICU. To prevent these complications, endotracheal intubation is regarded as a standard of care for the patient with a GCS score < 9 following severe head injury.[1] In the ED, the preferred approach for endotracheal intubation is rapid sequence intubation (RSI), a technique which combines the rapid administration of both sedation and a paralysing drug (suxamethonium), followed by immediate endotracheal intubation.[2] Although RSI is

Correspondence: Dr Stephen Bernard, Medical Director Air-Ambulance Victoria, Nomad Street, Essendon Airport, Victoria 3041, Australia. Email: stephen.bernard@dhs.vic.gov.au

Stephen Bernard, MBBS FACEM, Medical Director; Karen Smith, BSc (Hons), Diploma Epidemiology and Biostatistics, Senior Researcher; Shane Foster, MICA Cert., MICA Flight Paramedic; Phillip Hogan, MICA Cert., Team Manager; Ian Patrick, B. Paramedic Studies, MICA Cert, ASM Manager, Clinical Operations.

an approved protocol in some emergency medical services in North America,[3] ambulance services in Australia have not previously endorsed this approach because of concerns about failed intubation, unrecognized oesophageal intubation, skills teaching, skills maintenance and lack of proven benefit.[4]

In the aero-medical setting, transport of patients with severe head injury presents additional issues compared with road transport. There may be difficult access to the patient during flight for airway monitoring and the performance of emergency procedures. Also, transport times to definitive care are generally longer than road-based services.

In 1999, a protocol that allowed RSI by ambulance paramedics for patients with severe head injury was introduced into the Helicopter Emergency Medical Service (HEMS) in Victoria, Australia. The aim of this study was to determine the success rate and physiological effects of rapid sequence intubation in patients with severe head injury performed by paramedics on the HEMS.

Methods

This study was a retrospective review of ambulance medical records of patients with severe head injury attended at the scene by an ambulance paramedic on the HEMS between November 1999 and February 2002 (inclusive). The HEMS consists of three helicopters, each staffed by a pilot, attendant and one ambulance paramedic who has additional training in advanced life support and aviation medicine. Clinical protocols are medically determined and authorized without on-line consultation. One helicopter is based in Melbourne and responds to calls between 40 km and 250 km from Melbourne. Another is based 150 km south-east of Melbourne and responds to calls in the eastern region of Victoria. The third helicopter, which commenced operations in July 2001, is based 150 km north-west of Melbourne and responds to calls in the north and west of the state.

A protocol for prehospital RSI (Table 1) and a failed intubation drill (Fig. 1) were adapted from a previously published protocol.[2] A training program was developed which consisted of lectures on suxamethonium pharmacology, scenario training of the failed intubation drill, and practical experience using the laryngeal mask airway and RSI in the operating theatre. Cricothyroidotomy using a needle/guide-wire technique was taught using a Min-Trach II™ (Portex Ltd, Hythe,

Table 1. Rapid sequence intubation algorithm

Rapid sequence intubation algorithm
Pre-oxygenation with 100% oxygen
Intravenous access
Monitoring: (ECG, pulse oximetry, blood pressure, end-tidal carbon dioxide
Draw-up and label drugs
Administer: Morphine/midazolam 0.1 mg/kg, Suxamethonium 1.5 mg/kg, Atropine for heart rate < 60/min
Laryngoscopy
Endotracheal Intubation
Check position of ETT (clinical checks, capnography wave form, air aspiration test)
Secure ETT with tapes
Administer pancuronium 0.1 mg/kg and repeat as required
Commence morphine/midazolam infusion 0.1 mg/kg/h via syringe pump
Orogastric tube
Connect to ventilator (100% oxygen/tidal volume 10 mL/kg, adjust rate for end-tidal CO_2 35 mmHg)

ETT, endotracheal tube.

UK) cricothyroidotomy kit on a Laerdal™ mannikin (Laerdal, Huntingdale, Vic., Australia).

The use of RSI was authorized in patients without consultation if the GCS score was < 9, but consultation with a physician at the adult or paediatric destination hospital was required for patients with GCS scores between 10 and 12. Adult patients were transported to the Alfred Hospital and paediatric patients to the Royal Children's Hospital, both near the centre of Melbourne. The patient care records were collected by one of the authors (SB) and data on demographics, vital signs and procedures were extracted.

The view at laryngoscopy was recorded as grades 1–4 according to the scale of Cormack and Lehane[5] where Grade 1 indicates that the larynx is readily visible, Grade 2 indicates that the posterior larynx only is seen, Grade 3 indicates that the epiglottis only is seen and in a Grade 4 view the epiglottis cannot be visualized.

The fluid therapy for suspected hypovolaemia consisted of the administration of Hartmanns solution and Haemaccel®, which is administered in equal volumes of 500 mL boluses and repeated as required. As part of a separate study, patients with both hypotension and GCS < 9 received 250 mL of a blinded study fluid (either 7.5% hypertonic saline or Hartmanns solution).

Statistical analysis was undertaken using the commercial statistics package, Stata.[6] The changes in

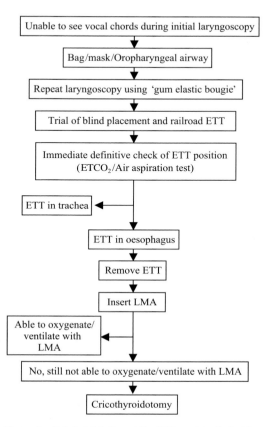

Unable to see vocal chords during initial laryngoscopy

↓

Bag/mask/Oropharyngeal airway

↓

Repeat laryngoscopy using 'gum elastic bougie'

↓

Trial of blind placement and railroad ETT

↓

Immediate definitive check of ETT position (ETCO₂/Air aspiration test)

ETT in trachea ←

ETT in oesophagus

↓

Remove ETT

↓

Insert LMA

Able to oxygenate/ventilate with LMA ←

No, still not able to oxygenate/ventilate with LMA

↓

Cricothyroidotomy

Figure 1. Failed intubation drill. ETT, endotracheal tube; ETCO$_2$, end-tidal CO$_2$; LMA, laryngeal mask airway.

Table 2. Demographics of the subjects studied to determine the success rate and physiological effects of rapid sequence intubation in patients with severe head injury performed by paramedics on the Helicopter Emergency Medical Service

Category	Number of subjects (%)
n	110 (100)
Age	32.3 ± 17.3 years
Male sex	81 (73.6)
Mechanism of the injury:	
Motor vehicle occupant	75 (68.2)
Motorcyclist	10 (9.1)
Pedestrian	12 (10.9)
Fall	9 (8.2)
Assault	2 (1.8)
Gunshot wound	1 (1.0)
Fall from horse	1 (1.0)
Total	110 (100)
GCS prior to RSI:	
3	20 (18.0)
4	5 (5.0)
5	4 (4.0)
6	16 (14.0)
7	24 (22.0)
8	20 (18.0)
9	12 (10.0)
10	1 (1.0)
11	2 (2.0)
12	2 (2.0)
13	1 (1.0)
Not recorded	3 (3.0)
Total	110 (100)

GCS, Glasgow coma scale; RSI, rapid sequence intubation.

continuous variables including vital signs were compared using ANOVA. A $P < 0.05$ was considered significant.

The training, implementation and data collection relating to the RSI protocol were approved by the Medical Standards Committee of the Metropolitan Ambulance Service.

Results

There were 122 patients with severe head injury attended at the scene of the crash by an ambulance paramedic on the HEMS during the study period. In 11 patients, endotracheal intubation was possible without pharmacological assistance because of deep coma and absent airway reflexes. In one patient (age 3 months), the paramedic elected to transport the patient without intubation. The remaining 110 patients had intact airway reflexes and underwent RSI. The demographics of these patients are shown in Table 2.

Most patients (99/110) had a Grade 1 view at laryngoscopy. In six patients, the view was Grade 2 and in five patients the view at laryngoscopy was Grade 3. Successful intubation was not achieved in three of the five patients with a Grade 3 view. Two of these patients were managed using bag/mask ventilation with oxygen followed by laryngeal mask airway insertion. Both patients arrived at the hospital with satisfactory oxygenation and ventilation, as measured by pulse oximetry and capnography. One patient was found to have a pharyngeal haematoma and required intubation using a fibre-optic technique.

Table 3. Vitals signs before and after rapid sequence intubation (RSI), mid-flight and on arrival at hospital

	Pre-RSI	Post-RSI	Mid-flight	Arrival
n	110	110	109	109
SBP mmHg	117 (36)	123 (28)*	129 (28)*	130 (25)*
Pulse/minute	105 (25)	113 (21)*	114 (22)*	110 (21)*
ETCO$_2$ mmHg	N/A	37 (16–68)†	32 (21–65)†	33 (17–45)†
Oxygen	93 (9)	97 (6) ‡	99 (3)‡	99 (3)‡

*Saturation percentage. Values given as means (± standard deviation) except ETCO$_2$ which is presented as median and range due to a non-parametric distribution. *P < 0.05 compared with preintubation. †P < 0.05 compared with post RSI; ‡insufficient preintubation data for postintubation statistical analysis. ETCO$_2$, end-tidal carbon dioxide; N/A, not available; SBP, systolic blood pressure.*

The other patient was found to have a large epiglottis and was intubated using a long-blade laryngoscope, with the epiglottis lifted directly. A third patient was unable to be intubated in the field, and was also unable to be satisfactorily ventilated using a laryngeal mask airway. Therefore, cricothyroidotomy was attempted and, although a guidewire was placed through the criciothyroid membrane into the trachea, the cricothyroidotomy tube was unable to be passed over the guidewire. There was transient oxygen desaturation, however, the patient resumed spontaneous respirations and subsequently made an excellent neurological recovery.

There was one patient who underwent RSI but died at the scene prior to transport. In this patient, minimal sedation had been administered and position of the endotracheal tube had been confirmed in the trachea by clinical checks with the oesophageal detector device and capnography prior to cardiac arrest. The patient failed to respond to vigorous fluid therapy and exclusion of a tension pneumothoraces. In comparison, four of 11 patients intubated without drugs died at the scene despite fluid resuscitation.

In one patient, intravenous access was lost immediately after RSI and attempts to replace this access were initially unsuccessful. The patient was extubated following the return of a cough reflex and spontaneous respirations. The patient was subsequently re-intubated after successful placement of another intravenous cannula.

The vital signs of the 110 patients immediately before and after RSI, mid-flight (109 patients) and on arrival at the trauma centre (109 patients) are shown in Table 3. These data show that systolic blood pressure was increased after RSI in most patients. In three patients, hypertension developed (BP > 160 mmHg) and was successfully treated with additional sedation. Hypotension occurred in 34 patients (31%) during ambulance care. There were 27 patients (25%) who

were hypotensive prior to RSI, 12 of these remained hypotensive immediately after RSI and 11 were still hypotensive on arrival at hospital despite vigorous intravenous fluid therapy. In seven other patients, transient hypotension occurred immediately following RSI. The patients with hypotension received a mean of 2075 mL of fluid, compared with patients without hypotension who received a mean of 950 mL of fluid.

An initial pulse oximetry reading was not able to be recorded in 33/110 (30%) patients, either because the patient was restless, or because they had poor peripheral perfusion. Where an accurate reading was possible (77 patients), hypoxaemia (oxygen saturation < 90%) was present in 17/77 (22%) patients. Only one patient was hypoxaemic on arrival at hospital. This patient was thought to have suffered severe aspiration pneumonitis prior to RSI.

In 17/110 patients, the position of the endotracheal tube was confirmed using a disposable qualitative device (EasyCap®, Nellcor-Puriton-Bennett, Pleasanton, Cal, USA). For the remaining 93 patients, the initial end-tidal carbon dioxide level immediately following RSI was > 45 mmHg in 19/93 (20%). This was corrected into the normal range in all patients by hospital arrival. There were no other apparent complications of RSI, such as aspiration during the procedure, unrecognized oesophageal intubation or accidental extubation.

The mean doses of midazolam and morphine were 7.1 mg (± 2.0) each. Only one patient required the administration of atropine for bradycardia (heart rate < 60/min).

The mean HEMS dispatch to scene arrival time was 25 min, scene arrival to arrival at patient 5 min, scene time 31 min (for 88 non-trapped patients) and flight time to hospital 23 min There were 22 patients who were still trapped at HEMS arrival and these patients had a mean scene time of 54 min. The time at scene included time for travel of the patient to the aircraft, patient loading and engine warm-up prior to take-off.

Discussion

It is recommended that patients with severe head injury undergo endotracheal intubation as soon as possible following injury.[1] However, it is uncertain whether intubation should be performed in the field by ambulance paramedics or in the ED by physicians.[4] The perceived difficulty with prehospital intubation is the cost and logistics of both initial training and skills maintenance to enable ambulance paramedics to undertake this procedure safely. When airway reflexes are present, the assistance of a muscle relaxant is required. However, failed intubation in the pharmacologically paralysed patient or unrecognized oesophageal intubation could worsen outcome or prove fatal.

Our study demonstrates that appropriately trained paramedics in an Australian helicopter emergency medical service are able to perform RSI in patients with severe head injury with a high success rate (97%), and that this procedure is associated with improvements in oxygenation, ventilation and blood pressure. When intubation was unsuccessful, a failed intubation drill including use of the laryngeal mask airway or cricothyroidotomy prevented an adverse outcome.

This study also confirms that secondary insults are common in patients with severe head injury, with an incidence of 25% having hypotension, 22% having low oxygen saturation and 20% having hypercarbia when these were first measured.

It is unclear from either this study or other studies in the literature whether prehospital intubation improves outcome. In a non-randomized study of 671 patients with severe head injury, prehospital intubation (without RSI) was associated with a decrease in mortality rate from 56% to 36%.[7] On the other hand, a retrospective study by Murray *et al.* compared 714 patients with severe head injury who were not able to be intubated with 81 patients who were able to be intubated.[8] The mortality rate was 43% in the unintubated patients compared with 81% of the intubated patients. Following multivariate analysis for gender, GCS, injury severity score, transport mode and mechanism of injury, there was a significant increase in mortality risk associated with prehospital intubation. However, no patient in this study received RSI.

A prospective, randomized controlled, study of prehospital intubation of paediatric patients also found that intubation was not associated with improved outcome.[9] However, paralysing drugs were not used to facilitate intubation and 43% of patients randomized to intubation were not able to be intubated. The small number of patients with severe head injury in this study also limited the conclusions that could be drawn from the findings.

There is evidence that RSI can be used safely in the prehospital setting. One review of 1657 prehospital intubations using RSI (in an American emergency medical service) showed that there was successful intubation in 95.5%.[10] The patients with failed intubation were successfully managed with other means (i.e. bag/mask ventilation or cricothyroidotomy). Unrecognized oesophageal intubation occurred in 0.3% of patients prior to the introduction of capnography. Another study also found equivalent success rates with prehospital RSI and ED RSI.[11]

In Australia, there have been two studies of patients with severe head injury transported by helicopter services. One study compared outcomes in patients with major trauma in two aero-medical emergency medical services, one staffed by paramedics who were not authorized to use RSI and the other by experienced physicians.[12] In the paramedic service, 39% of patients with GCS < 9 were able to be intubated (without drug therapy) compared with 100% (using RSI) on the physician staffed service. This difference was thought to contribute to the increased mortality rate reported in the paramedic-staffed service. In another study of the HEMS in Victoria, ambulance clinical practice guidelines at that time allowed the use of sedation alone (morphine plus diazepam) for endotracheal intubation.[13] Intubation was possible in 94% of patients; however, a gag reflex was still present in 46%. In addition, 22% of patients had a change in blood pressure of > 20 mmHg. This approach was regarded as unsatisfactory, since increased intracranial pressure (due to gagging/coughing) and a decreased blood pressure (due to large doses of sedation) could result in a significant decrease in cerebral perfusion pressure and secondary brain injury.[14]

Conclusion

Our study has a number of limitations. First, the retrospective design means that some complications may have occurred but were not noted in the ambulance patient care record. Second, the study did not include analysis of chest radiography in the ED to determine the incidence of endo-bronchial intubation. Finally, without a control group, no conclusions can be drawn on whether RSI improved the outcomes of these patients.

Nevertheless, we have demonstrated that paramedics in a helicopter emergency medical service may successfully undertake RSI in patients with severe head injury and this is associated with improvements in blood pressure, oxygen saturation and end-tidal carbon dioxide levels. Therefore, we propose that further studies of RSI by road-based ambulance paramedics be undertaken, and that RSI be tested against current ambulance practice to determine which approach has the best outcome.

Accepted 10 July 2002

References

1. The Brain Trauma Foundation. The American Association of Neurological Surgeons. The Joint Section on Neurotrauma and Critical Care. Resuscitation of blood pressure and oxygenation. *J. Neurotrauma* 2000; **17**: 471–8.

2. Bernard SA. Advanced airway management. In: Cameron P, Jelinek G, Kelly AM (eds). *A Textbook of Adult Emergency Medicine*. London: Churchill Livingstone, 2000; 16–20.

3. McDonald CC, Bailey B. Out-of-hospital use of neuromuscular-blocking agents in the United States. *Prehospital Emerg. Care* 1998; **2**: 29–32.

4. Liberman M, Mulder D, Sampalis J. Advanced or basic life support for trauma: Meta-analysis and critical review of the literature. *J. Trauma* 2000; **49**: 584–99.

5. Cormack RS, Lehane J. Difficult intubation in obstetrics. *Anaesthesia* 1984; **39**: 1105–11.

6. StataCorp. Stata statistical software. In: *Release 6, College Station, Stata Corporation*; 1999.

7. Winchell RJ, Hoyt DB. Endotracheal intubation in the field improves survival in patients with severe head injury. *Arch. Surg.* 1997; **132**: 592–7.

8. Murray JA, Demetriades D, Berne TV *et al.* Prehospital intubation in patients with severe head injury. *J. Trauma* 2000; **49**: 1065–70.

9. Gausche M, Lewis RJ, Stratton SJ *et al.* Effect of out-of-hospital pediatric endotracheal intubation on survival and neurological outcome. *JAMA* 2000; **283**: 783–90.

10. Wayne MA, Friedland E. Prehospital use of succinylcholine: A 20 year review. *Prehospital Emerg. Care* 1999; **3**: 107–9.

11. Sloane C, Vilke GM, Chan TC *et al.* Rapid sequence intubation in the field versus hospital in trauma patients. *J. Emerg. Med.* 2000; **19**: 259–64.

12. Garner A, Rashford S, Lee A *et al.* Addition of physicians to paramedic helicopter services decreases blunt trauma mortality. *ANZ J. Surg.* 1999; **69**: 697–701.

13. Sams J, Kelly AM. Use of an emergency sedation protocol to assist intubation in helicopter patient retrieval in Victoria. *Emerg. Med.* 1999; **11**: 84–9.

14. Chesnut RM. Avoidance of hypotension: Conditio sine qua non of successful severe head-injury management. *J. Trauma* 1997; **42**: S4–S9.

The Journal of **TRAUMA** *Injury, Infection, and Critical Care*

The Effect of Paramedic Rapid Sequence Intubation on Outcome in Patients with Severe Traumatic Brain Injury

Daniel P. Davis, MD, David B. Hoyt, MD, Mel Ochs, MD, Dale Fortlage, BA, Troy Holbrook, PhD, Lawrence K. Marshall, MD, and Peter Rosen, MD

Objective: To evaluate the effect of paramedic rapid sequence intubation (RSI) on outcome in patients with severe traumatic brain injury.

Methods: Adult major trauma victims were prospectively enrolled over two years using the following inclusion criteria: Glasgow Coma Scale (GCS) 3–8, suspected head injury by mechanism or physical examination, transport time > 10," and inability to intubate without RSI. Midazolam and succinylcholine were administered before laryngoscopy; rocuronium was given after tube placement was confirmed using physical examination, capnometry, syringe aspiration, and pulse oximetry. The Combitube was used as a salvage airway device. For this analysis, trial patients were excluded for absence of a head injury (Head/Neck AIS score < 2), failure to fulfill major trauma outcome study criteria, unsuccessful intubation or Combitube insertion, or death in the field or in the resuscitation suite within 30" of arrival. Each study patient was hand matched to three nonintubated historical controls from our trauma registry using the following parameters: age, sex, mechanism of injury, trauma center, and AIS score for each body system. Controls were excluded for Head/Neck AIS defined by a c-spine injury or death in the field or in the resuscitation suite within 30" of arrival. χ^2, odds ratios, and logistic regression were used to investigate the impact of RSI on the primary outcome measures of mortality and incidence of a "good outcome," defined as discharge to home, rehabilitation, psychiatric facility, jail, or signing out against medical advice.

Results: A total of 209 trial patients were hand matched to 627 controls. The groups were similar with regard to all matching parameters, admission vital signs, frequency of specific head injury diagnoses, and incidence of invasive procedures. Mortality was significantly increased in the trial cohort versus controls for all patients (33.0% versus 24.2%, $p < 0.05$) and in those with Head/Neck AIS scores of 3 or greater (41.1% versus 30.3%, $p < 0.05$). The incidence of a "good outcome" was lower in the trial cohort versus controls (45.5% versus 57.9%, $p < 0.01$). Factors that may have contributed to the increase in mortality include transient hypoxia, inadvertent hyperventilation, and longer scene times associated with the RSI procedure.

Conclusion: Paramedic RSI protocols to facilitate intubation of head-injured patients were associated with an increase in mortality and decrease in good outcomes versus matched historical controls.

Key Words: Brain injury, Head trauma, Intubation, Paramedics, RSI outcome.

J Trauma. 2003;54:444–453.

Prehospital hypoxia and hypotension have been associated with increased mortality in patients with severe traumatic brain injury.[1–4] Aggressive prehospital airway protocols including rapid sequence intubation (RSI) by aeromedical crews and specially trained paramedics have been instituted in many systems to improve intubation success.[5–16] Multiple reports have demonstrated an increase in intubation success rates and minimal reported complications with prehospital RSI.[13,17–19] Our own experience with paramedic RSI includes successful airway management in 99% of patients, including 84% with orotracheal intubation (OTI) and 15% with Combitube (The Kendall Company, Mansfield, MA, U.S.A.) insertion (CTI) and no unrecognized esophageal intubations. As a result, airway management success rates for severely head-injured patients in our prehospital system increased from 39% in the pre-trial period to 86% during the trial.[20,21]

Despite improvements in prehospital intubation success with aggressive airway protocols, there have been relatively few attempts to document the effect on outcome. In a retrospective cohort analysis, Winchell and Hoyt reported a 10-percent absolute survival benefit from paramedic intubation without the use of neuromuscular blocking agents.[8] Garner et al. documented improved survival in trauma patients treated by aeromedical physicians versus patients transported by ground paramedics; however, there was not an independent benefit from intubation, with the improvements in survival likely a result of early blood administration.[22] The goal of this analysis was to explore the impact of paramedic RSI on outcome in severely head-injured patients.

PATIENTS AND METHODS
Design

Subjects were prospectively enrolled and hand-matched to historical nonintubated controls from the same prehospital

Submitted for publication October 13, 2002.

Accepted for publication December 5, 2002.

Copyright © 2003 by Lippincott Williams & Wilkins, Inc.

From the Department of Emergency Medicine (D.D., P.R.), Department of Surgery, Division of Trauma, Department of Surgery (D.H., D.F., T.H.), and Division of Neurosurgery (L.M.), UC San Diego, and San Diego County Emergency Medical Services (M.O.), San Diego, California, U.S.A.

Presented at the 61st Annual Meeting of the American Association for the Surgery of Trauma, September 26–28, 2002, Orlando, Florida.

Support for this project was received from the Society for Academic Emergency Medicine.

Address for correspondence: Daniel Davis, MD, UCSD Emergency Medicine, 200 West Arbor Drive, #8676, San Diego, California, U.S.A. 92103-8676

DOI: 10.1097/01.TA.0000053396.02126.CD

Table 1 Rapid Sequence Intubation Medication Protocols Used During the Trial

Medication	Small 80–140 lbs. (35–63 kg)	Average 141–225 lbs. (63–100 kg)	Large >225 lbs. (>100 kg)
Midazolam	2 mg	2.5 mg	3.0 mg
Succinylcholine	4 ml (80 mg)	6 ml (120 mg)	8 ml (160 mg)
Rocuronium	4 ml (40 mg)	6 ml (60 mg)	8 ml (80 mg)
Morphine	2 mg every 10 min for "stress response" (SBP >140 mmHg, HR >100 BPM)		

SBP, systolic blood pressure; HR, heart rate; BPM, beats per minute.

system. The enrollment period for this analysis was from November 1998 through November 2000. Waiver of consent was granted by the California State EMS Authority and from the Investigational Review Board for each participating institution.

Setting and prehospital system

San Diego County has a population of almost 3 million with an area of 4,261 square miles. Advanced life support is provided by 12 different agencies, with all but one agency participating in the trial. There are approximately 110,000–120,000 emergency transports each year of which about 30% are trauma related. Responses for major trauma victims are two-tiered, with a minimum of two paramedics dispatched to each call. In addition, aeromedical crews consisting of a flight nurse and either a specially trained flight paramedic or Emergency Medicine resident respond from two bases at the request of ground crews. Five designated adult trauma centers receive all major trauma victims. For this trial, paramedics attended an 8-hour training course to learn the RSI procedure and medications and Glasgow Coma Scale (GCS) scoring and to review ventilation procedures and CTI techniques.

Subjects

The target population for this study was adult major trauma victims with severe head injuries. Inclusion criteria were as follows: 1) apparent age 18 years or older; 2) major trauma victim per county protocols; 3) suspected head injury by mechanism or physical examination findings; 4) GCS score 3–8; and 5) estimated time for transport to the resuscitation suite 10 minutes or greater. Paramedics first attempted intubation without RSI medications. Patients were enrolled in the trial if intubation attempts were unsuccessful or in the presence of a clenched jaw or airway reflexes inhibiting laryngoscope blade insertion. Patients were excluded for inability to achieve intravenous (IV) access or if cardiopulmonary resuscitation (CPR) were required before administration of RSI medications.

Interventions

Trial patients were monitored with three-lead ECG and pulse oximetry and were pre-oxygenated for a minimum of 60 seconds using a non-rebreather mask. If oxygen saturation remained below 95%, then bag-valve-mask (BVM) ventilations were instituted before medication administration. Mi-

dazolam was administered for sedation if SBP was 120 mm Hg or greater; succinylcholine was used to achieve neuromuscular blockade. Once tube position was confirmed, rocuronium was administered to maintain paralysis during transport. Additional midazolam was administered after 30 minutes if SBP remained 120 mm Hg or greater. Morphine sulfate was given for a "stress response," defined as a SBP greater than 140 mm Hg and a heart rate greater than 100 BPM. A simplified, weight-based dosing system was used (Table 1).

Paramedics then attempted endotracheal (ET) intubation; after a maximum of three unsuccessful ET intubation attempts, CTI was mandated. The anterior cervical collar was loosened and manual in-line stabilization held during all intubation attempts; the Sellick maneuver was performed upon administration of medications. Tube position was confirmed using direct visualization, bilateral breath sounds and absent gastric air sounds, qualitative capnometry, syringe aspiration, and pulse oximetry. If all intubation attempts were unsuccessful, further laryngoscopy attempts were abandoned and BVM ventilation performed until spontaneous respirations resumed. Paramedics were taught standard ventilation parameters of 12 breaths per minute and a tidal volume of 800 cc; practice with a stopwatch and spirometer was incorporated into the training session. During the second year of the trial, one agency instituted the use of continuous end-tidal CO_2 (ETCO2) monitoring; paramedics from this agency were instructed to adjust ventilation parameters to target an ETCO2 value of 30–35 mm Hg and avoid values of less than 25 mm Hg.

Data collection

Prehospital data are entered into an electronic database of all EMS patients transported in San Diego County. In addition, a field worksheet served as both a protocol guide and a data collection tool for RSI trial patients. One of the principal investigators was contacted immediately following delivery of each RSI patient for a 15-minute telephone debriefing to confirm proper GCS score calculation based on reported physical examination findings and obtain additional data regarding prehospital course. Finally, data for each trauma patient meeting major trauma outcome study criteria are entered into a county trauma registry; hospital admission summaries, including head injury diagnosis and invasive procedures, are available for most registry patients. Abstracted data were entered into an Excel (Microsoft, Redmond, WA, U.S.A.) database for further analysis.

Matched Controls

The primary objective for this analysis was to determine the effect of prehospital RSI on outcome in severely head-injured patients. Exclusion criteria for this analysis included: 1) inability to be intubated (OTI or CTI) by prehospital personnel following administration of RSI mediations; 2) absence of a head injury (Head/Neck AIS less than 2); 3) Head/Neck AIS defined by a neck injury; 4) failure to fulfill MTOS criteria; and 5) death in the field or resuscitation suite within 30 minutes of arrival. Each of the remaining study patients was hand matched to three nonintubated historical controls from the county trauma registry using the following criteria: age, sex, mechanism of injury, trauma center, ISS, Head/Neck AIS score, Face AIS score, Chest AIS score, Abdomen AIS score, Extremities AIS score, and Skin AIS score. The two individuals responsible for matching were blinded to outcome. Controls were excluded for death in the field or within 30 minutes of arrival in the resuscitation suite and if the Head/Neck AIS score were defined by a cervical spine injury rather than a head injury. Although the registry includes patients from the past 10 years, preference was given to selecting patients from the preceding 5 years.

Data Analysis

Patients were pooled into a trial cohort and a control cohort for analysis. The primary outcome measures were mortality, defined as death before hospital discharge, and incidence of a "good outcome," which included discharge to home, rehabilitation, psychiatric facility, jail, or signing out against medical advice. In our trauma system, discharge to rehabilitation requires anticipation of some degree of functional recovery and is not used for patients expected to require long-term support. In addition, a small group of trial patients underwent primary management by aeromedical crews, with RSI medications administered by the flight paramedic and the intubation performed by the flight nurse. Separate analyses were performed after exclusion of these patients and their matched controls and for patients with more severe head injuries (Head/Neck AIS of 3 or greater).

Trial patients and controls were also compared with regard to each of the matching parameters: presenting vital signs, scene times, arterial blood gas (ABG) values, and serum ethanol. Available admission summaries were used to determine the incidence of head injury diagnoses (contusion/intraparenchymal hemorrhage, subdural hematoma, epidural hematoma, cerebral edema, subarachnoid hemorrhage, and skull fracture) and the incidence of invasive procedures (craniotomy, laparotomy, and thoracotomy). Finally, the mortality impact of hyperventilation, multiple intubation attempts, OTI versus CTI, and location of the RSI procedure (on scene versus en route) were explored using actual versus predicted

mortality, calculated for each trial patient using the mean survival for the three matched controls. The median arrival pCO_2 value was used as a threshold to defined hyperventilation.

Statistical analysis

The primary outcome measures of mortality and a "good outcome" as defined above were analyzed using χ^2, with the association between outcome and RSI status quantified using the odds ratio. In addition, logistic regression was used to investigate the association between mortality and RSI status, controlling for age, sex, Head/Neck AIS, Chest AIS, Abdomen AIS, scene time, and admission SBP. Rank sum and t-testing were used when appropriate to compare RSI patients and controls with regard to matching and clinical parameters. Descriptive statistics were used to explore the impact of hyperventilation, multiple intubation attempts, CTI versus OTI, and location of RSI on outcome. Statistical significance was attributed to a p-value less than 0.05. Statistical calculations were performed using SAS/STAT (SAS Institute Inc., Cary, NC, U.S.A.).

RESULTS

During the 2-year study period, 250 patients were enrolled in the trial. Two patients were intubated before paramedic contact but received midazolam and rocuronium en route to the trauma center; another patient was taken to a nontrauma center and was excluded from further analysis. In addition, four patients did not receive succinylcholine per the study protocol. One began vomiting after receiving midazolam and did not receive succinylcholine, while a second patient mistakenly received a tenth dose of succinylcholine and never achieved relaxation. In the other two cases, paramedics arrived at the trauma center before administering succinylcholine and elected not to continue the procedure. All four patients underwent successful intubation in the trauma resuscitation suite. Of the remaining 243 patients, 242 (99%) underwent successful airway management, including 212 (87%) OTI patients and 30 (12%) CTI patients.

Of the 242 patients undergoing successful airway management, 10 were excluded for a Head/Neck AIS score less than 2, and 16 were excluded for not fulfilling MTOS criteria. One of these had a myocardial infarction while driving and hit a parked car at low speed, but was unresponsive due to a dysrhythmia. Another patient sustained an arterial gas embolism while scuba diving, and four others were ultimately determined to have nontraumatic intracranial hemorrhage. In addition, three patients were declared dead in the field and four died in the resuscitation suite within 30 minutes of arrival; all seven had severe multi-system traumatic injuries and were felt to be nonsalvageable (Table 2).

The remaining 209 patients were hand-matched to 627 controls from the county trauma registry. Matching parameters are displayed in Table 3 with no significant differences observed between the two groups. Scene time, arrival vital

Table 2 Trial Patients Excluded from This Analysis Using Criteria Determined a Priori

Reason for Exclusion	No. of Patients
Protocol violation	5
No succinylcholine given	4
Inappropriate succinylcholine dose	1
Did not meet MTOS criteria	16
Discharge <24 hours	10
Cerebrovascular accident	4
Myocardial infarction with dysrhythmia	1
Arterial gas embolism while scuba diving	1
Trauma victim with Head/Neck AIS score of 0 or 1	10
Death in resuscitation suite <30 minutes after arrival	4
Death in field	3
Intubated prior to paramedic contact	1
Taken to nontrauma center	1
Failure to intubate	1

MTOS, major trauma outcome study; AIS, abbreviated injury score.

signs and ABG values, and serum ethanol are displayed in Table 4. Of note, scene times were longer, arrival pO2 values higher, and arrival pCO2 values lower in the RSI cohort. In addition, the incidence of inadvertent severe hyperventilation, defined as an arrival pCO2 value of 25 mm Hg or less was significantly higher in the RSI cohort versus controls. Admission summaries were available for a total of 561 control patients (83%) and 173 RSI patients (83%). Head injury diagnoses and the incidence of invasive procedures were similar between the two cohorts (Table 5).

With regard to the primary outcome measures, there was a statistically significant increase in mortality and decrease in "good outcomes" in the RSI cohort versus controls; this was also true for patients with Head/Neck AIS scores of 3 or greater and after exclusion of six aeromedical patients and their matched controls (Table 6). There were no statistically significant differences between the groups with regard to the number of days in the ICU or total hospital length of stay. Logistic regression revealed a statistically significant effect on mortality for RSI status (trial patient versus control) controlling for all other variables modeled (Table 7). The hospital day of death was similar between the two groups, with a bimodal distribution of deaths on hospital days 1 or 2 and on hospital days 4 and 5 (Fig. 1).

Using the predicted mortality defined above, we explored the effect of inadvertent hyperventilation on outcome using the median arrival pCO2 value of 33 mm Hg as a threshold. Hyperventilated RSI patients (pCO2 less than the median value of 33 mm Hg) appeared to have an increased mortality when compared with nonhyperventilated RSI patients; the groups were similar with regard to other parameters (Table 8). A similar increase in mortality was observed for patients undergoing a single (versus multiple) intubation attempt, CTI patients, and those intubated en route (Tables 9–11).

Table 3 Age, Sex, Mechanism of Injury, Abbreviated Injury Scores, and ISS for the RSI Cohort (n = 209) Versus Pooled Matched Controls (n = 627)

Parameter	Controls (%)	RSI (%)	p Value
Demographics			
Age (years)	36.8	37.1	0.629
Male sex	81	81	0.918
Mechanism of injury			
Motor vehicle accident	39	39	0.935
Fall	23	23	0.924
Assault	8	8	0.884
Bike accident	5	5	0.858
Motorcycle accident	5	5	0.852
Peds vs. auto	10	10	0.894
Gunshot wound	5	5	0.852
Found down	3	3	0.811
Other	2	2	0.771
Abbreviated injury scores			
Head/Neck (mean)	3.92	3.91	0.930
2	20	20	0.881
3	14	15	0.777
4	19	20	0.880
5	45	44	0.779
6	1	1	1.000
Face (mean)	0.56	0.62	0.519
0	72	69	0.451
1–2	22	25	0.417
3+	6	6	0.864
Chest (mean)	1.01	1.24	0.155
0	69	63	0.137
1–3	20	22	0.552
4–6	12	15	0.206
Abdomen (mean)	0.58	0.67	0.473
0	80	77	0.325
1–3	15	17	0.509
4–6	12	15	0.206
Extremities (mean)	0.98	0.92	0.692
0	61	62	0.870
1–2	18	20	0.605
3+	21	18	0.157
Skin (mean)	0.96	0.96	0.917
0	18	23	0.157
1+	82	77	0.157
ISS (mean)	26.3	27.6	0.222

RSI, rapid sequence intubation; ISS, injury severity score.

DISCUSSION

Despite multiple studies documenting the adverse effects of hypoxia on outcome in patients with severe traumatic brain injury, there is a paucity of evidence to suggest that an aggressive approach to airway management leads to improvements in mortality. Here we document a mortality increase in patients undergoing paramedic RSI when compared with matched historical controls from the same prehospital system. This increase was most profound in patients with higher Head/Neck AIS scores, with mortality of 41.1% in the RSI cohort versus 30.3% in controls. In addition, there was a corresponding decrease in "good outcomes" for the RSI cohort, defined as discharge to home, rehabilitation, psychiatric facility, jail, or signing out against medical advice.

Table 4 Scene Time, Arrival SBP, Arterial Blood Gas Values, and Serum Ethanol for RSI Patients (n = 209) Versus Pooled Matched Controls (n = 627)

	Controls	RSI	p Value
Minutes on scene (mean)	16.4	22.8	<0.0001
Systolic blood pressure			
Mean (mmHg)	138.4	138.6	0.907
SBP ≤90 mmHg (%)	6.4	6.8	1.000
ABG data			
pH (mean)	7.36	7.36	0.850
pO2 (mean in mmHg)	216	315	<0.0001
pCO2 (mean in mmHg)	38.3	34.9	<0.0001
Base excess (mean)	−3.4	−4.3	0.002
Inadvertent hyperventilation (%)	8.0	15.4	0.014
Mean serum ethanol (mg/dl)	101	111	0.656

RSI, rapid sequence intubation; SBP, systolic blood pressure; ABG, arterial blood gas.

The critical challenge in interpreting these results is to determine whether the mortality increase in the RSI cohort is an unanticipated consequence of the procedure itself or instead represents some inequity between the trial patients and their matched controls. The two cohorts appeared to be equivalent on all parameters we measured, including age, sex, AIS values for each body system, ISS, arrival SBP, head injury diagnoses, and incidence of invasive procedures. Absent from our matching criteria, however, was GCS score, which can be predictive of outcome in head-injured patients. Before the trial, field GCS was not consistently calculated and when obtained reflected arrival GCS rather than immediately upon arrival. Admission GCS values were available for the control cohort but were recorded as a value of 3 or omitted from most trial patients, as they were paralyzed and intubated. We felt that the use of individual body system AIS scores provided more consistent and accurate matching. In addition, the head injury diagnoses and incidence of invasive procedures were similar between the two groups.

Table 5 Incidence of Head Injury Diagnoses and Invasive Procedures from Review of Available Admission Summaries for Controls (n = 521) and RSI Patients (n = 173)

Outcome measure	Controls (%)	RSI (%)	p Value
Head injury diagnoses			
Contusion/intraparenchymal hematoma	53.6	53.8	0.967
Subdural hematoma	40.1	42.8	0.598
Epidural hematoma	27.6	25.4	0.641
Skull fracture	38.2	34.7	0.461
Subarachnoid hemorrhage	38.2	46.2	0.075
Cerebral edema	24.8	27.7	0.497
Invasive procedures			
Craniotomy	22.6	17.9	0.228
Laparotomy	8.8	11.0	0.489
Thoracotomy	2.3	4.0	0.343

RSI, rapid sequence intubation.

Table 6 Primary Outcome Measures for the RSI Cohort (n = 209) Versus Controls (n = 627)

Outcome measure	Controls (%)	RSI (%)	Odds ratio
Mortality			
All patients	24.2	33.0	1.6 (1.1–2.2)*
Head/neck AIS 3 or greater	30.3	41.1	1.6 (1.1–2.3)*
Non-aeromedical	24.3	33.0	1.6 (1.1–2.2)*
Good outcome¶			
All patients	57.9	45.5	1.6 (1.2–2.3)†
Head/neck AIS 3 or greater	49.3	37.5	1.6 (1.1–2.3)†
Non-aeromedical	58.3	45.8	1.7 (1.2–2.3)‡
Total days in ICU	6.0	7.1	NS
Total days in hospital	14.5	12.2	NS

* $p < 0.05$
† $p < 0.01$
‡ $p < 0.001$
¶ Odds ratios calculated with "good outcome" as the reference variable.
RSI, rapid sequence intubation; AIS, abbreviated injury scale; ICU, intensive care unit; NS, non-significant.

We excluded patients intubated in the field without RSI medications from both the trial and control cohorts. If a higher percentage of these patients existed before the trial, this would create a selection bias toward more neurologically intact patients in the pool of patients from which we selected the controls. Our previous analysis reveals the opposite to be true, however, with a higher percentage of patients intubated without RSI medications during the trial.[21] This would have selected more neurologically intact patients for inclusion in the trial, although the impact is likely small. We also considered whether the RSI procedure and early intubation merely prolonged life for a few hours in patients who otherwise might have died in the field or the resuscitation suite and been excluded from analysis. Figure 1 demonstrates that the hospital day of death was similar between the two cohorts, with no increase in deaths on hospital days 1 and 2 observed in the RSI cohort.

If the differences in outcome represent a true negative effect of paramedic RSI, then it is imperative that factors potentially responsible for the increase in mortality be thoroughly investigated. One possibility concerns the incidence of inadvertent hyperventilation, which was significantly higher in the RSI group. This phenomenon has been docu-

Table 7 Logistic Regression Model Investigating the Impact of RSI and Head/Neck AIS on Mortality for All Patients Together (n = 836)

Parameter	Adjusted OR*	p Value
RSI	1.6	0.03
Head/Neck AIS	73.0	<0.0001

* Adjusted for age, sex, Chest AIS, Abdomen AIS, admission SBP, and scene time.
RSI, rapid sequence intubation; AIS, abbreviated injury scale; OR, odds ratio.

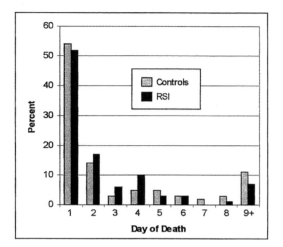

Fig. 1. *Hospital day of death for RSI patients (n = 209) controls (n = 627).*

mented previously with both paramedics and aeromedical crews, but the impact on outcome is unknown.[23] While hyperventilated and nonhyperventilated patients appeared to be equivalent on all parameters measured, the mortality was higher for RSI patients with lower arrival pCO2 values versus their predicted outcomes as compared with those with higher pCO2 values. The introduction of ETCO2 monitors may allow more accurate control of ventilation and avoid potential complications related to hyperventilation.

The introduction of ETCO2 monitors also allowed pulse oximetry data to be recorded and stored for later analysis.

Table 8 Effect of Hyperventilation on Outcome Using the Median Arrival pCO2 Value of 33 mmHg as Threshold

	RSI patients with pCO2 <33 mmHg (n = 100)	RSI patients with pCO2 ≥33 mmHg (n = 101)
Mortality		
RSI cohort (%)	39.0	25.7
Predicted (%)	27.3	23.1
Years of age (mean)	38.2	35.4
Sex (% male)	79.0	83.2
Abbreviated Injury Scores (mean)		
Head/Neck	3.98	3.80
Face	0.55	0.72
Chest	0.91	1.55
Abdomen	0.66	0.70
Extremities	0.77	1.13
Skin	0.99	0.94
ISS (mean)	26.6	28.5
Mean arrival SBP (mean)	134.0	142.6

RSI, rapid sequence intubation; ISS, injury severity score; SBP, systolic blood pressure.

Table 9 Effect of Multiple Intubation Attempts on Outcome

	RSI patients with single intubation attempt (n = 123)	RSI patients with multiple intubation attempts (n = 86)
Mortality		
RSI cohort (%)	37.4	26.7
Predicted (%)	23.6	25.2
Years of age (mean)	36.1	38.5
Sex (% male)	80.5	80.2
Abbreviated Injury Scores (mean)		
Head/Neck	3.86	3.99
Face	0.56	0.70
Chest	1.17	1.35
Abdomen	0.72	0.58
Extremities	0.86	1.01
Skin	0.95	0.97
ISS (mean)	27.7	27.5
Mean arrival SBP (mean)	133.0	146.4

RSI, rapid sequence intubation; ISS, injury severity score; SBP, systolic blood pressure.

Using these data, we documented transient hypoxia in over half of patients undergoing ETCO2 monitoring, with many of these developing concurrent bradycardia.[24] This is substantially higher than the 15–20% incidence of hypoxia reported for trauma intubations performed in the resuscitation suite.[25] While the impact of transient hypoxemia on head injury is unknown, the concurrent hemodynamic instability we observed suggests a systemic effect that may be even more significant to the injured brain.

Patients with multiple intubation attempts appeared to do slightly better than those intubated on the first attempt. While this may seem counterintuitive, patients undergoing multiple attempts at intubation may have been monitored more closely, with paramedics quickly abandoning an attempt at

Table 10 Effect of CTI Versus OTI on Outcome

	RSI patients with Combitube insertion (n = 28)	RSI patients with orotracheal intubation (n = 181)
Mortality		
RSI cohort (%)	39.3	32.0
Predicted (%)	26.2	23.9
Years of age (mean)	39.0	36.9
Sex (% male)	89.0	79.0
Abbreviated Injury Scores (mean)		
Head/Neck	4.14	3.89
Face	1.00	0.57
Chest	1.46	1.20
Abdomen	0.82	0.64
Extremities	0.96	0.91
Skin	0.93	0.96
ISS (mean)	29.6	27.3
Mean arrival SBP (mean)	136.4	137.3

CTI, Combitube insertion; OTI, orotracheal intubation; RSI, rapid sequence intubation; ISS, injury severity score; SBP, systolic blood pressure.

Table 11 **Effect of Performing RSI on Scene Versus En Route on Outcome**

	Patients undergoing RSI on scene (n = 140)	Patients undergoing RSI en route (n = 69)
Mortality		
RSI cohort (%)	31.4	36.2
Predicted (%)	25.7	21.3
Years of age (mean)	36.4	38.6
Sex (% male)	80.7	79.7
Abbreviated Injury Scores (mean)		
Head/Neck	3.99	3.77
Face	0.66	0.52
Chest	1.32	1.09
Abdomen	0.72	0.55
Extremities	0.94	0.90
Skin	0.95	0.97
ISS (mean)	28.6	25.7
Mean arrival SBP (mean)	140.5	134.4

RSI, rapid sequence intubation; ISS, injury severity score; SBP, systolic blood pressure.

the first sign of desaturation or hemodynamic instability. This is difficult to extract from these data, and further analysis of the ETCO2 recordings may lead to a better understanding of this phenomenon. Patients undergoing CTI appeared to have slightly poorer outcomes; however, these patients appeared to have more severe injuries. Nevertheless, the effect of CTI on hemodynamics, cerebral perfusion, and ICP has not been documented.

Another factor that may play a role in outcome is the delay in transport associated with RSI, especially when the procedure was performed on scene rather than en route. The impact of this delay is unclear, especially since the incidence of significant chest or abdominal trauma that might lead to hemorrhagic shock was relatively low. Nevertheless, rapid transport to a designated trauma center has been demonstrated to improve outcome, and the impact of additional prehospital delays cannot be discounted. We observed slightly worse outcomes in patients undergoing RSI en route. The initial SBP was lower in this group, possibly explaining the decision to transport sooner and potentially accounting for some of the increase in mortality. There may also have been additional challenges and complications with the RSI procedure performed in the back of a moving ambulance.

It is important to note the relatively high number of trial patients (n = 67) ultimately determined to have either a minor concussion or no head injury. A small number of these had significant nontraumatic disease that might also have benefited from aggressive airway management, including hemorrhagic stroke and cardiac dysrhythmia; however, most of these had normal neurologic examinations upon arrival at the trauma center. Fortunately, none had complications related to the RSI procedure or early intubation, but their existence underscores the need to consider the impact of RSI protocols on patient selection. Ultimately, additional variables, such as hypoxia or the absence of airway reflexes, may

need to be incorporated into the decision regarding the use of RSI. It is also interesting to note that the mean arrival pO2 value for nonintubated controls was 216 mm Hg, which is well into the therapeutic range.

It is important to consider the limitations of this analysis in interpreting these results. While the RSI and control cohorts appeared to be identically matched, there may have been other parameters we did not consider that could account for the increase in mortality in the RSI cohort. Ultimately, a randomized trial is warranted to further investigate the impact of prehospital RSI on outcome in head-injured patients. Based on these data, the San Diego Paramedic RSI Trial was suspended until an avoidable cause for the increase in mortality could be determined.

Several important factors were identified that warrant further attention in other prehospital systems considering paramedic RSI. The high incidence of inadvertent hyperventilation and transient hypoxia and their potentially detrimental effect on outcome suggest that the procedure should be performed only after intensive training and with use of sophisticated monitoring devices. In addition, the use of GCS alone as indication for RSI may be too limited, and other factors, such as loss of airway reflexes or hypoxia despite supplemental oxygen, deserve further investigation as indictors of the need for invasive airway management. Finally, the experience of the paramedics performing RSI should be considered. The paramedics in our prehospital system have significant experience with advanced airway skills; however, performing RSI every one or two years may lead to a decay in familiarity with the RSI procedure. Ultimately, a small group of specially trained paramedics with significant airway experience and ongoing training may be safer and more efficient in applying RSI to the prehospital environment.

CONCLUSIONS

Paramedic RSI improves intubation success rates but is associated with an increase in mortality and decrease in "good outcomes" when compared with hand-matched controls. These differences may reflect inherent inequities between the two groups, although they appeared similar on all parameters we measured. Alternatively, the increase in mortality may be related to inadvertent hyperventilation, transient hypoxic episodes, and prolonged scene times associated with the RSI procedure.

ACKNOWLEDGMENTS

The authors gratefully acknowledge the contributions made by the San Diego County Base Hospital and Trauma Departments, American Medical Response, San Diego Medical Services Enterprise, Mercy Air, county flight nurses, the RSI Educational Task Force and trainers, paramedic provider agency coordinators, Palomar and Southwestern Colleges, the County of San Diego Division of EMS bio-statistical team, the California EMS Authority, and especially the paramedics throughout San Diego County whose enthusiastic support made the study possible. The authors particularly note David Bailey, RN, Ginger Ochs, RN, Gina Anderson, RN, Kelly Forman, RN, and Mark Angeloni, RN, for their training contributions.

REFERENCES

1. Chesnut RM, Marshall LF, Klauber MR, et al. The role of secondary brain injury in determining outcome from severe head injury. *J Trauma*. 1993;34:216–222.

2. Pigula FA, Wald SL, Shackford SR, Vane DW. The effect of hypotension and hypoxia on children with severe head injuries. *J Pediatr Surg*. 1993;28:310–316.

3. Stocchetti N, Furlan A, Volta F. Hypoxemia and arterial hypotension at the accident scene in head injury. *J Trauma*. 1996;40:764–767.

4. Kokoska ER, Smith GS, Pittman T, Weber TR. Early hypotension worsens neurological outcome in pediatric patients with moderately severe head trauma. *J Pediatr Surg*. 1998;33:333–338.

5. Smith JP, Bodai BI. The urban paramedic's scope of practice. *JAMA*. 1985;253:544–548.

6. Aprahamian C, Darin JC, Thompson BM, Mateer JR, Tucker JF. Traumatic cardiac arrest: Scope of paramedic services. *Ann Emerg Med*. 1985;14:583–586.

7. Hatley T, Ma OJ, Weaver N, Strong D. Flight paramedic scope of practice: Current level and breadth. *J Emerg Med*. 1998;16:731–735.

8. Winchell RJ, Hoyt DB. Endotracheal intubation in the field improves survival in patients with severe head injury. *Trauma Research and Education Foundation of San Diego Archives of Surgery*. 1997;132:592–597.

9. McDonald CC, Bailey B. Out-of-hospital use of neuromuscular-blocking agents in the United States. *Prehosp Emerg Care*. 1998;2:29–32.

10. Karch SB, Lewis T, Young S, Hales D, Ho CH. Field intubation of trauma patients: Complications, indications, and outcomes. *Am J Emerg Med*. 1996;14:617–619.

11. Doran JV, Tortella BJ, Drivet WJ, Lavery RF. Factors influencing successful intubation in the prehospital setting. *Prehospital and Disaster Medicine*. 1995;10(4):259–64.

12. Katz SH, Falk JL. Misplaced endotracheal tubes by paramedics in an urban emergency medical services system. *Ann Emerg Med*. 2001;37:32–37.

13. Sing RF, Reilly PM, Rotondo MF, Lynch MJ, McCans JP, Schwab CW. Out-of-hospital rapid-sequence induction for intubation of the pediatric patient. *Acad Emerg Med*. 1996;3:41–45.

14. Syverud SA, Borron SW, Storer DL, et al. Prehospital use of neuromuscular blocking agents in a helicopter ambulance program. *Ann Emerg Med*. 1988;17:236–242.

15. Vilke GM, Hoyt DB, Epperson M, Fortlage D, Hutton KC, Rosen P. Intubation techniques in the helicopter. *J Emerg Med*. 1994;12:217–224.

16. Falcone RE, Herron H, Dean B, Werman H. Emergency scene endotracheal intubation before and after the introduction of a rapid sequence induction protocol. *Air Med J*. 1996;15:163–167.

17. Wayne MA, Friedland E. Prehospital use of succinylcholine: A 20-year review. *Prehosp Emerg Care*. 1999;3:107–109.

18. Pace SA, Fuller FP. Out-of-hospital succinylcholine-assisted endotracheal intubation by paramedics. *Ann Emerg Med*. 2000;35:568–572.

19. Hedges JR, Dronen SC, Feero S, Hawkins S, Syverud SA, Shultz B. Succinylcholine-assisted intubations in prehospital care. *Ann Emerg Med*. 1988;17:469–472.

20. Ochs M, Davis DP, Hoyt DB, Bailey D, Marshall LM, Rosen P. Paramedic-performed rapid sequence intubation of severely head-injured patients. *Ann Emerg Med*. 2002;40:159–167.

21. Davis DP, Ochs M, Hoyt DB, Marshall LM, Rosen P. Standing Orders for Paramedic Rapid Sequence Intubation Improves Prehospital Intubation Success in Severe Head-injured Patients. *J Trauma*. (in press).

22. Garner A, Crooks J, Lee A, Bishop R. Efficacy of prehospital critical care teams for severe blunt head injury in the Australian setting. *Injury*. 2001;32:455–460.

23. Thomas SH, Orf J, Wedel SK, Conn AK. Hyperventilation in traumatic brain injury patients: Inconsistency between consensus guidelines and clinical practice. *J Trauma*. 2002;52:47–53.

24. Doney M, Dunford J, Ochs M. Transient hypoxemia during rapid sequence intubation by paramedics for closed head injury [abstract]. *Prehosp Emerg Care*. 2002;6:148–149.

25. Omert L, Yeaney W, Mizikowski S, Protetch J. Role of the emergency medicine physician in airway management of the trauma patient. *J Trauma*. 2001;51:1065–8.

DISCUSSION

Dr. David H. Livingston (Newark, New Jersey): This excellently written study covers an important topic—does allowing field paramedics to perform RSI in the field improve outcome with patients with traumatic brain injury? There is really little to offer these patients other than removing mass lesions and avoiding hypotension and hypoxia and probably hypercapnia. Thus, it would seem logical that intubating them in the field would be beneficial. However, despite really a very nice, elegant study and an analysis that tortured the data until it would confess, the authors could not show a benefit of RSI in patients with RSI who did worse no matter how they cut the data.

As this argument is currently played out in my own home state of New Jersey and elsewhere, I can assure the audience that I used this data to try to quash paramedic RSI in my own state.

The authors began to articulate some of the issues here—unrecognized hypoxia during the intubation and over aggressive ventilation that resulted in some of the respiratory parameters. Clearly, this study also shows that the time in the field was increased in patients undergoing RSI. In the argument between the scoop and run and stay and play, scoop and run once again wins out.

Lastly, the study again demonstrates the concept: just because you can do something, maybe you shouldn't. During my fellowship, Dr. Richardson kept referring to this as if the only tool you have is a hammer, and everything begins to look like a nail. Thus, if we give the paramedics the ability to intubate, they will want to intubate again and again.

Who do you think really was benefiting from this procedure if there was anybody benefiting from it in the field?

In our own estimation, looking at 1,200 RSIs in our emergency department, maybe 10 to 15 or 20 percent of patients, max, would benefit; thus, a lot of people would be intubated in the field, and you'd wonder whether they should.

How much did this whole program cost? If you were going to go forward to do this, how do you keep the paramedics recurrently training, especially if they are only doing one or two a year, and how much does this cost in an ongoing program?

Lastly, given your data, I have a big question. Are you going to pull this from the paramedics in the field? Clearly, your data at a 3:1 cohort match looks pretty good that patients are doing worse.

Dr. Daniel P. Davis (San Diego, California): The principal investigators met 2 days after the data was analyzed, and they decided to suspend the trial until we could determine whether the increase in mortality was a true effect of RSI or whether there was some error in the way that we had done the matching. In continuing to analyze the data for the subsequent 6 months, we could not come up with anything to suggest that these 2 groups were inappropriately matched. Thus, we have not reinitiated the trial, and within the past month, the California State EMS Board voted to discontinue the trial.

We have discussed performing a different trial in the future that might utilize a select group of medics who undergo more specific training. That introduces the question about the cost of training. For this trial, all medics who went through the training course were eligible to perform RSI regardless of how many intubations they had accumulated. Over 500 medics went through an 8-hour training course for which they were compensated. Instructors were also paid, and course materials, including home study aids, were supplied to the medics. In addition, there were administrative costs, not to mention the cost of medication and equipment. I'm sure you can imagine that it's a fairly substantial endeavor. Of note, specific refresher courses were not required, bringing up the issue of a decay in skills with time.

We are looking at the number of medication and protocol violations and have noticed that they appear to increase as a function of time following the initial training module. Anecdotally, medics have told me that they feel less comfortable with the procedure several years out from the training course, especially if they hadn't been involved with an RSI in the interim. The data collection sheet also served as a cheat sheet for the medics, helping guide them through the procedure, but anybody who has performed RSI knows that it's infinitely more complex than something that can be performed from a cookbook.

As far as who benefits from the procedure, we have not yet identified a particular RSI subgroup that does better than their matched controls. This analysis pooled all RSI patients and all controls, breaking the line between each patient and his or her matched controls. Future analyses may retain this link to investigate the role of certain parameters in determining outcome and defining patients who may benefit from RSI. I think there were many patients who were doing just fine on their own and did not require RSI, opposed to patients who were hypoxic despite supplemental oxygen or bag valve mass ventilation and likely benefitted from intubation.

Dr. Richard J. Mullins (Portland, Oregon): I think the authors have carefully examined the value of rapid sequence intubation and demonstrated that, with it, patients had improved survival in the prehospital phase in the later time period.

If you improve airway management in patients with brain injury, one consequence should be that more patients will survive to be admitted to your trauma center, but some will still expire because of their lethal brain injury. Vital statistics records regarding patients who die of unintended injury generally show that 60 to 80 percent of blunt trauma patients expire at the scene.

My question relates to your measure of survival. Would not 6-month survival be a better indicator in brain-injured patients of whether you benefited patients with your process of rapid sequence intubation?

Dr. Daniel P. Davis (San Diego, California): Originally, one arm of this study was intended to use the Glasgow Outcome Scale to determine long-term outcome, however it quickly became apparent that the only patients that we could find consistently were the dead ones, and the lack of follow-up became the fatal flaw for that part of the study. We were limited to using data available from the trauma registry, which meant that once a patient left the hospital, they were lost to follow up.

Dr. James W. Davis (Fresno, California): I, too, commend the authors on this study, however I'm wondering if the outcomes aren't even worse than were suggested. Should the failure to intubate be part of an intent to treat analysis? In other words, you can make an airway a whole lot worse by attempting to instrument it, and then, if you don't get that airway, those patients may, indeed, do worse. Further, you excluded all your early deaths and your scene deaths. Did any of those patients have an unrecognized or a missed intubation or an esophageal intubation?

Dr. Daniel P. Davis (San Diego, California): Those are excellent questions, and I think that those questions would have even more relevance if we had demonstrated a benefit with RSI. If we had performed an intent to treat analysis, we most likely would have observed even greater mortality in the RSI group.

Of the 7 deaths that occurred in the field or within 30 minutes of arrival, all had severe multi-system injuries that were deemed to be nonsurvivable. It was not thought to be the RSI procedure itself that lead to the death. Conversely, there were patients who did not have significant injuries but in whom the medics had difficulty establishing an airway, with hypoxic injury noted on CT scans, although none resulted in death.

Dr. Arthur L. Trask (Vienna, Virginia): The scenario that you described is a reverse of what we have done in Fairfax, Virginia, where there is only a select group, probably 10 or fewer, that are allowed to do RSI. They are all related to the helicopter services in that area. Our statistics are totally the opposite of what yours are, and that is we don't do RSI if they're less than 10 minutes from the hospital, or if they can be there with the scoop and run technique. However, in those areas where we can't get there because of the traffic and so on, the helicopter comes in, picks them up, and does RSI. The mortality statistics in those patients were significantly different, 30 percent improved mortality in our RSI group. The training of 10 people is a lot different than the training of 600, and that's why we have kept it to that size group.

Dr. Daniel P. Davis (San Diego, California): I agree. I think that the future of prehospital RSI is going to require more intensive training for a select group of people, be they air medical teams or a small group of specially trained medics who may or may not work in every prehospital system.

Our enrollment criteria required that the transport time be an estimated 10 minutes or longer; thus "scoop and haul" was still the standard when closer to the trauma center.

Dr. Randal M. Chesnut (Portland, Oregon): This is a very nice study, and this methodology becomes quite definitely Class II when it reaches peer-reviewed publication. The question will then be when it generates a lot of discussion, to whom will this be not generalizable? In other words, San Diego is sort of a specific situation—the history of the trauma system, the set up of short transport times, etc. In what communities would this not be applicable? What does it take as a baseline to consider applying such an RSI protocol?

Dr. Daniel P. Davis (closing): In any city that was considering adding RSI to the scope of practice for all medics, I think this is going to give them significant pause. If the situation is such that a "strike team" of specially trained medics can be stationed at several locations in a particular city and quickly reach the scene to perform RSI, it may still be worth considering.

In southern California, where the cities are 50 to 100 or more miles wide, it's not feasible to have specially trained teams of medics who will require 30 to 45 minutes to get to any particular scene. In this scenario, air medical teams are the only viable option to perform RSI.

As far as paramedic RSI is concerned, i think it must be special trained "strike teams" stationed at various points in a city where they could easily get to any scene in a timely fashion. Even in such an idealized scenario, there is not enough evidence that early intubation improves outcome in traumatic brain injury.

Rapid Sequence Intubation

There are ways of identifying impending respiratory failure.

By Tracy Evans, MS, MPH, APRN, CCRN, CEN, and Patricia Carroll, MS, RN, BC, CEN, RRT

Emily Winters, 43, was admitted to the ICU yesterday, diagnosed with Guillain-Barré syndrome (GBS). Since admission, she has experienced increasing chest muscle paresthesia and difficulty in coughing.

The hospital staff knows Harry Gonzalez, 68, quite well. He has steroid-dependent chronic obstructive pulmonary disease (COPD), and is often admitted for exacerbations with and without pneumonia. He was admitted to the emergency department this morning after four days of increasing dyspnea at home. He has left lower lobe pneumonia.

Derek Chen, 23, fell off a mountain bike 14 hours ago. He was awake and alert when he arrived at the emergency department with retrograde amnesia and a possible loss of consciousness at the scene of the accident. After a thorough examination, the only clinical finding was a headache. The initial CT scan revealed a small, left-sided epidural hematoma and four hours later another scan showed no change. His neurologic examination remained normal, except for the headache. Six hours after arrival, he was admitted to the ICU for observation and frequent neurologic assessments.

Each of these patients has a different disease process, but they all have one thing in common: the risk of respiratory failure. With an understanding of the types of respiratory failure, a critical care nurse can quickly identify patients with impending respiratory failure so that intervention, such as rapid sequence intubation, can be carried out in relatively controlled, nonemergent conditions.

RECOGNIZING RESPIRATORY FAILURE

Respiratory failure has one or both of the following characteristics: failure of oxygen exchange manifested by hypoxemia, or failure of ventilation manifested by hypercapnia. A patient with type I respiratory failure has an abnormally low PaO_2,

with a $PaCO_2$ that is either low or normal. A patient with type II respiratory failure suffers from both hypoxemia and hypercapnia.[1] Be particularly alert to respiratory failure in patients with lung disease or acute lung injury, in patients in whom the respiratory center of the brain is depressed, in patients with neuromuscular disease, and in patients with musculoskeletal injury (such as a cervical spine injury) that can affect the respiratory muscles.

Generally, a patient diagnosed with acute respiratory failure meets two of the following criteria: acute dyspnea; PaO_2 less than 50 mmHg (FIO_2 0.21); $PaCO_2$ greater than 50 mmHg; and significant respiratory acidemia as shown by arterial pH. In assessing the patient, look for indicators of hypoxemia and hypercapnia, including: tachypnea, tachycardia, anxiety, restlessness, diaphoresis, slurred speech, altered mental status, and headache.

A physical assessment and laboratory analysis of arterial blood gases will reveal existing respiratory failure. This article will discuss additional nursing assessments that will identify patients who are *approaching* respiratory failure, before blood gas results indicate significant deterioration. Ms. Winters, Mr. Gonzalez, and Mr. Chen have come to the ED with disorders that may not necessarily lead to respiratory failure, but overlooked signs of distress could result in emergency intubation.

WITH NEUROMUSCULAR DISEASE

Ms. Winters' respirations are 38 breaths per minute and SpO_2 (pulse oximetry) is 93% on room air. The respiratory therapist has measured her forced vital capacity (FVC) and negative inspiratory force (NIF) every four hours. (The NIF provides information on the strength of the *respiratory muscles* against a maximal stimulus.[2] The FVC is a metered measurement of the patient's exhalation.) The last time it was checked, the FVC was only 1.0 L, reduced from a high point of 1.36 L on admission, and the NIF was only −20 mmHg. FVC should be greater than 15 ml/kg and the NIF less than (more negative) −25 mmHg.[3]

GBS is an acute, inflammatory, demyelinating disorder of the peripheral nervous system,[4] the clin-

Tracy Evans is the trauma coordinator at Norwalk Hospital, Norwalk, CT. Her mentor, Patricia Carroll, is a per-diem emergency department nurse at Manchester Memorial Hospital in Manchester, CT, and owner of Educational Medical Consultants in Meriden, CT.

ical course of which begins with distal paresthesia followed by lower extremity weakness and pain that take an ascending pathway. Respiratory failure, the most serious complication, is caused by the loss of motor innervation to respiratory muscles. Respiratory efforts are ineffective, breathing is shallow, and it's difficult for the patient to cough and clear secretions that can block the airway.

Because Ms. Winters has no history of lung disease, abnormalities in blood gases will be a late sign of impending respiratory failure. Her blood gas values may be normal at this point, because her elevated respiratory rate compensates for her decreased tidal volume. But if the FVC is decreasing and the NIF is low (less negative), there is impending respiratory failure. Incremental measurements of FVC and NIF will reveal whether values continue in a downward trend, which would indicate a progressive weakening of respiratory muscle function and the need for intubation and mechanical ventilation.

WITH PULMONARY DISEASE

Mr. Gonzalez's arterial blood gases are always abnormal, so "normal" values don't apply to his condition, which makes nursing assessment more challenging and more critical. A nurse must assess Mr. Gonzalez's blood gas results in light of *his* baseline at previous admissions, and not according to textbook values. An assessment of his breathing, stamina, and nutritional status will determine how long he can maintain his breathing without assistance. Because of the effort required to breathe, Mr. Gonzalez has had difficulty in swallowing and sleeping, and after four days of increasing dyspnea at home, he says that he's exhausted. He's using all of his accessory muscles to breathe, his posture is slumped, and he's slow to answer questions. Regardless of blood gas findings, he's experiencing impending respiratory failure. Often, COPD patients who have required ventilator support in the past can tell you when they are tiring and in need of mechanical breathing assistance.

WITH INCREASED INTRACRANIAL PRESSURE

Eight hours after his arrival, Mr. Chen's nurse asks for help. He is sleeping restlessly, he has a Cheyne-Stokes breathing pattern, and cannot be woken. His heart rate is 46 beats per minute, his blood pressure is 190/50 mmHg, and his right pupil is dilated. The ICP is compressing the pons and medulla, where the brain's respiratory centers are located. In addition, the decreased level of consciousness may compromise the airway because Mr. Chen will be unable to clear it of vomitus or secretions, and his tongue may be too relaxed and fall back. His blood gases are normal at the moment but, because of threatened airway compromise, he must be intubated.

RAPID SEQUENCE INTUBATION

Rapid sequence intubation (RSI), the cornerstone of emergency airway management, involves the rapid administration of a sedative agent and a neuromuscular blocking agent in order to facilitate intubation. The American Association of Critical Care Nurses' protocol on sedation and neuromuscular blockade in patients with acute respiratory failure states that the critical ethical issue is the provision of adequate sedation and analgesia before pharmacologic paralysis.[5] The objective of RSI is to intubate the conscious patient safely and with limited discomfort or pain. The therapeutic goal is the successful transition from a state of consciousness and respiratory distress to a state of unconsciousness with complete neuromuscular paralysis. Sedation must be a part of the process so that the patient is not both awake *and* paralyzed.

THE SIX Ps OF RSI[5]

Preparation. Evaluate the patient's need for intubation and assess factors that may make it difficult to achieve (such as obesity, trauma to the face or mouth, or scar tissue). The physician or nurse practitioner will choose appropriate induction, sedation, and paralytic drugs, and determine the need for premedication.

After notifying the respiratory therapist that a patient needs to be intubated, check the equipment. Remembering the acronym SOAPME (**s**uction, **o**xygen, **a**irway equipment, **p**harmacology, **m**onitoring **e**quipment) helps in the preparation of equipment for an intubation.[6]

Preoxygenation. Administer high levels of oxygen with a bag-valve-mask device for at least five minutes before intubation. The purpose of preoxygenation is to create an oxygen reserve so that blood levels will not drop despite a period of apnea during intubation. Preoxygenation should be performed concurrently with preparation and pretreatment.

Pretreatment. RSI is not free of risk, but premedication will help to mitigate possible complications.

Direct laryngoscopy will immediately cause an increase of ICP because of the reflex sympathetic response to mechanical stimulation of the larynx and trachea,[7] especially dangerous in patients at risk of stroke. Lidocaine is administered to reduce ICP[8]; it attenuates airway reaction and coughing that may occur as well during laryngoscopy and intubation.[7,9] The usual dose is 1 mg/kg IV.[10]

Esmolol, a beta-blocker, maintains cardiovascular stability during RSI, decreases myocardial oxygen demand, and reduces the risk of an increase of

Drugs Commonly Used During Rapid Sequence Intubation

Agent	Classification	Effects	Cautions/ Contraindications	Dose (IV)	Onset	Duration
Thiopental	Barbiturate	• Decreases CNS activity • Negative inotrope • Potent vasodilator • Releases histamine	• Asthma • State of shock	3 mg/kg	30 to 60 seconds	5 to 8 minutes
Ketamine	Phencyclidine derivative	• Dissociative anesthetic—profound analgesia but not unconsciousness • Airway reflexes preserved • Hemodynamic stability • Bronchodilation • Increases cerebral metabolic rate • Nightmares during emergence • Increases intragastric pressure • Increases oral secretions • Hypertonicity	• Head injury	1 to 2 mg/kg	30 to 60 seconds	10 to 15 minutes
Midazolam	Benzodiazepine	• Decreases CNS activity • Amnesia • Negative inotrope • Mild cerebroprotective effects	• State of shock	0.1 to 0.3 mg/kg	35 to 45 seconds	10 to 15 minutes
Fentanyl	Opiate	• Decreases CNS activity	• Variable dosing • Myasthenia gravis • Chest wall rigidity with rapid infusion	Up to 150 μg/ kg as required	45 to 60 seconds	30 to 60 minutes
Propofol	Sedative-hypnotic	• Cerebroprotective effects • Decreases MAP	• Ages 3 and older • State of shock • Allergies to eggs or soybean oil	2 to 2.5 mg/kg	10 to 20 seconds	10 to 15 minutes
Etomidate	Imidazole derivative	• Hemodynamic stability • Cerebroprotective effects • Cardioprotective effects		0.3 mg/kg	30 to 60 seconds	3 to 10 minutes

ICP. Doses of 100 mg and 200 mg are effective in reducing response.

Fentanyl has been found to be even more successful in attenuating the reflex sympathetic response to laryngoscopy. Research shows that fentanyl at 5 μg/kg limits heart rate increase more effectively than at 2 μg/kg.[8, 11] However, fentanyl is an opioid and increasingly higher doses may result in respiratory depression after the procedure.

Combining fentanyl and esmolol is an effective way of use lowering the doses of each. The administration of 2 μg/kg of fentanyl with 100 mg to 150 mg of esmolol limits increase in heart rate and mean arterial pressure while minimizing adverse effects.[8, 11]

Neuromuscular Blocking Agents Commonly Used During Rapid Sequence Intubation

Agent	Classification	Contraindications	Dose (IV)	Onset	Duration	Possible Adverse Effects
Succinylcholine	Depolarizing	• Severe burns • Major crush injuries • Denervation syndromes or major nerve or spinal cord injury • Severe abdominal sepsis	1 to 2 mg/kg	30 to 60 seconds	4 to 6 minutes	• Malignant hyperthermia • Increased ICP • Increased intraocular pressure • Arrhythmias
Rapacuronium	Nondepolarizing	• Myasthenia gravis	1.5 mg/kg	1.5 to 2 minutes	12 to 16 minutes	• Hypotension • Tachycardia • Bradycardia
Vecuronium	Nondepolarizing	• Myasthenia gravis	0.1 mg/kg	2 to 4 minutes	30 to 40 minutes	• Malignant hyperthermia
Pancuronium	Nondepolarizing	• Myasthenia gravis	0.1 mg/kg	4 to 6 minutes	120 to 180 minutes	• Tachycardia • Hypertension • Increased peripheral vascular resistance
Rocuronium	Nondepolarizing	• Myasthenia gravis	0.8 to 1.2 mg/kg	1 to 2 minutes	14 to 16 minutes	• Tachycardia • Hypertension • Increased peripheral vascular resistance

Note: dosing is that used for RSI, not for all indications.

SOURCES:

Wadbrook PS. Advances in airway pharmacology. Emerging trends and evolving controversy. *Emerg Med Clin North Am* 2000;18(4):767-88.

Strange GR, [et al.], editors. APLS: *the pediatric emergency medicine course*. 3rd ed. Dallas (TX): American College of Emergency Physicians, American Academy of Pediatrics; 1998.

Spratto G, Woods AL. PDR *nurse's drug handbook*. Montvale (NJ): Medical Economics; 2000.

Atropine reduces secretions and vagal stimulation. During intubation, stimulation of the laryngeal nerve, a branch of the vagus nerve, may result in bradycardia. Vagal stimulation may also occur as a result of hypoxia, or as a side effect of succinylcholine (a paralytic drug used in the RSI procedure). Because bradycardia is more pronounced in infants and children, atropine must be administered to children under two years old prior to intubation. The recommended dose of atropine is 0.02mg/kg; minimal doses are 0.1 mg in infants and 0.5 mg in adolescents and adults.[6]

Paralysis with sedation. The patient must be adequately sedated before being paralyzed, to prevent anxiety. Do not administer a sedative or a paralytic until all equipment is set up, checked, and ready for the procedure. Only short-acting paralytic drugs should be used during RSI because it's dangerous to give a long-acting paralytic *before* the airway is secured. (If a patient is paralyzed and then can't be intubated, the patient should be able to breathe spontaneously, however shallowly, as soon as possible. After successful intubation, a long-term sedative and a long-acting paralytic may be administered, as indicated by the patient's condition.) The doses of pancuronium and vecuronium in *Neuromuscular Blocking Agents Commonly Used During Rapid Sequence Intubation* are small doses used to reduce fasciculation that may be caused by succinylcholine. These doses will not achieve long-term paralysis.

Placement of the endotracheal tube. During intubation, be ready with a rigid suction tip should the patient's airway need to be cleared to make the vocal cords visible. The person performing the intubation may ask you to perform Sellick's maneuver, the pressing of the cricoid cartilage posteriorly, resulting in the compression of the esophagus to reduce the risk of vomiting and aspiration. The cricoid pressure is held until the person intubating the patient asks for its release. After intubation, collaborate with the respiratory therapist in listening to breath sounds in the axillary area on each side, monitoring SpO_2 and $ETCO_2$, (end-tidal carbon dioxide), and securing the tube.

Post-intubation management. After intubation, connect the patient to the ventilator. After four to six minutes, when the neuromuscular blockade has worn off, assess how well the patient's breathing synchronizes with the machine. Review the patient's blood gases. Evaluate his need for additional sedation or paralysis, and discuss your findings with the physician or nurse practitioner. Also, confirm that a chest X-ray has been ordered to evaluate tube position.

PATIENTS CAN BREATHE EASY

Ms. Winters required intubation because of progressive muscle weakness caused by GBS. She was premedicated with esmolol to mitigate an increase of ICP and any cardiovascular effects. She was sedated with propofol, a sedative-hypnotic, to depress laryngeal reflexes and induce amnesia, and with fentanyl for analgesia.[9] A neuromuscular blocking agent was not used because she had muscle weakness, and it's risky to use paralytics in patients with neuromuscular disease. She was assessed for signs of anxiety and breathing that might have been asynchronous with the ventilator, which could indicate the need for additional sedation.

Mr. Gonzalez required intubation because of COPD exacerbation. His blood pressure was 100/60 mmHg and he had no history of cardiovascular disease. He was pre-medicated with lidocaine to blunt the increase of ICP, reducing the risk of stroke. Esmolol, a beta-blocker contraindicated in patients with reactive airway disease, wasn't used. Mr. Gonzalez was sedated with ketamine because it promotes bronchodilation through sympathetic stimulation without the histamine release characteristic of a barbiturate (thiopental, for example).[9] Ketamine, however, can cause disturbing hallucinations, particularly in adults, so he was also given midazolam to induce amnesia. Succinylcholine was used for paralysis because of its rapid onset and

short duration. Once recovered from sedation and the intubation drugs, propofol was administered for rest and to facilitate ventilator synchrony for 24 hours. Chemical paralysis in steroid-dependent patients is discouraged because of the risk of prolonged muscle weakness after discontinuation.[12]

Mr. Chen required intubation because of a sudden, dramatic deterioration of neurologic status. He was sedated with etomidate because of its cerebroprotective qualities, quick onset, and short duration.[9] Succinylcholine was used for paralysis for the same reasons. Once Mr. Chen recovered from the sedation and intubation drugs, and the endotracheal tube placement was confirmed, the sedation was continued with propofol because it, too, has cerebroprotective effects. Because he remained restless despite sedation, paralysis was continued with vecuronium.

Critical care nurses are usually the first to identify impending respiratory failure. And once it's established that a patient requires intubation, the nurse is the ideal clinician to assist with RSI. In drawing up the medications, preparing equipment, assisting during the procedure, collaborating with the health care team, and monitoring the patient afterward, the nurse is essential.▼

REFERENCES

1. Bone RC, [et al.], editors. *Pulmonary and critical care medicine.* St. Louis: Mosby; 1997.
2. Scanlan CL, et al., editors. *Egan's fundamentals of respiratory care.* 7th ed. St. Louis: Mosby; 1999.
3. Hornick D, et al. *Management of hypercapnic respiratory failure* [online]. Virtual Hospital, Univeristy of Iowa Health Care. 1999. http://www.vh.org/Providers/Lectures/EmergencyMed/ARF/ManagementHypercapnic.html.
4. Kinney MR, [et al.]. *AACN's clinical reference for critical care nursing.* 4th ed. St. Louis: Mosby; 1998.
5. Luer JM. *Sedation and neuromuscular blockade in patients with acute respiratory failure.* Aliso Viejo (CA): American Association of Critical Care Nurses; 1998.
6. Strange GR, [et al.], editors. *APLS: the pediatric emergency medicine course.* 3rd ed. Dallas (TX): American College of Emergency Physicians, American Academy of Pediatrics; 1998.
7. Lev R, Rosen P. Prophylactic lidocaine use preintubation: a review. *J Emerg Med* 1994;12(4):499-506.
8. Rodricks MB, Deutschman CS. Emergent airway management. Indications and methods in the face of confounding conditions. *Crit Care Clin* 2000;16(3):389-409.
9. Wadbrook PS. Advances in airway pharmacology. Emerging trends and evolving controversy. *Emerg Med Clin North Am* 2000;18(4):767-88.
10. Spratto G, Woods AL. *PDR nurse's drug handbook.* Montvale (NJ): Medical Economics; 2000.
11. Abrams KJ. Airway management and mechanical ventilation. *New Horiz* 1995;3(3):479-87.
12. Behbehani NA, et al. Myopathy following mechanical ventilation for acute severe asthma: the role of muscle relaxants and corticosteroids. *Chest* 1999;115(6):1627-31.

28 REFERENCES

1 Cormack, R.S., Lehane, J. (1984). Difficult tracheal intubation in obstetrics. Anaesthesia, 39, (11): 1105-11.

2 Mallampati SR, Gatt SP, Gugino LD, Desai SP, Waraksa B, Freiburger D, Liu PL. (1985). A clinical sign to predict difficult intubation: a prospective study. Canadian Anaesthetists Society Journal. 32: 429-434.

3 Takahata, O., Kubota, M., Mamiya K., Akama, Y., Nozaka, T., Matsumoto, H., Ogawa, H. (1997). The efficacy of the 'BURP' manouver during a difficult laryngoscopy. Anesthesia & Analgesia, 84, (2): 419-421.

4 Sellick, Brian A. (1961). "Cricoid pressure to control regurgitation of stomach contents during induction of anaesthesia". The Lancet 278, (7199): 404–406.

5 Pollard, R.J., Lobato, E.B. (1985). Endotracheal location verified reliably by cuff palpation. Anaesthesia & Analgesia, 81. 135-138.

6 Alspaugh, D.M., Sartorelli, K., Shackford, S.R., Okum, E.J., Osler, T. (2000). Prehospital resuscitation with phenylephrine in uncontrolled hemorrhagic shock and brain injury. Journal of Trauma, Infection and Critical Care, 48, (5): 851–863.

Ambulance Victoria. (2009). Clinical Practice Guidelines (2009 ed.). Melbourne; Ambulance Victoria.

Moyle, J.T.B. (2002). Pulse Oximetry (2nd ed.). London: BMJ Books.

Novametrix. (2000). Sensors and Patient Connections. In Tidal Wave Sp – User Manual (5th revision ed., pp. 27–40). Walingford: Novametrix Medical Systems Inc.

Philips Medical Systems. (2007). Heartstart MRx Instructor Guide (3rd ed.). Andover: Koninklijke Philips Electronics N.V.

Ambulance Victoria

MICA Paramedic
Rapid Sequence Intubation
Accreditation

Information Package

July 2009

3rd edition

RAPID SEQUENCE INTUBATION
INFORMATION PACKAGE

This information package is the Clinical Support Officer (CSO) assessment procedure for Rapid Sequence Intubation (RSI) accreditation in Ambulance Victoria (AV).

This RSI Accreditation Information Package will be made available to all MICA Paramedics. All relevant responses and direct answers necessary for completion of the RSI assessment are based upon information contained in the AV Metropolitan MICA Continuing Professional Education 2002 (CPE) – Rapid Sequence Intubation handouts, the Novametrix Tidal Wave Sp Users Manual, the Phillips Heartstart MRx Cardiac Monitor User Manual, the AV Clinical Practice Guidelines (CPG), AV Clinical Work Instructions (CWI), and the RSI reference book (3rd Edition). MICA paramedics who commenced their MICA training after September 2002, received this content during the MICA course conducted by Monash University Department of Community Health & Paramedic Practice, and / or the MICA paramedic post 12-month on-road Study day, and / or a CSO provided RSI Update Information session conducted between June 2005 and January 2006.

The RSI reference book (3rd Edition) package has been made available to all MICA Paramedics in AV.

ASSESSMENT CATEGORIES

This assessment will consist of four components.

1. Use of Capnography
2. Rapid Sequence Intubation – preparation, procedure and successful intubation
3. Rapid Sequence Intubation – difficult / failed intubation drill
4. Drug Information

Follow the assessment guide for each category.

Fill in the assessment form as it relates to each category.

GRADES OF PERFORMANCE

Utilise the performance criteria items as the standard for assessing the candidates' performance.

There are three grades.

- Proficient
- Near Proficient
- Not Proficient

A candidate is Proficient if all Performance Criteria items are achieved.

A candidate is Near Proficient if all ⋆ items in the Performance Criteria are achieved, but other items have not been achieved.

A candidate is graded as Not Proficient if any starred item is not achieved.

ASSESSMENT REFERENCES

All assessment requirements are based upon information contained in the MICA Continuing Professional Education programme – Rapid Sequence Intubation handouts (or similar from the alternate sessions) the Novametrix Tidal Wave Sp Users Manual, the Phillips Heartstart MRx Cardiac Monitor User Manual, the AV Clinical Practice Guidelines, AV Clinical Work Instructions, the RSI reference book (3rd Edition), and the supporting video on RSI.

RECORDING THE ASSESSMENT

- Record the candidates' performance on the Assessment Report form.
- Copy forms, one copy to the candidate, the other copy to the Manager Education Services, Quality & Education Services Department.

ACCREDITATION RESULT

Proficiency must be demonstrated in all assessment categories prior to any authorisation to practice Rapid Sequence Intubation being granted.

A candidate who attains a Near Proficient or Not Proficient outcome will be required to be re-assessed in the areas were proficiency was not obtained within approximately two weeks.

If the re-assessment is deemed to be again Near Proficient or Not Proficient, the CSO will provide tutorial assistance followed by a further re-assessment in approximately two weeks time.

If a second re-assessment is deemed to be Near Proficient or Not Proficient, forward all details to the Manager Education Services, who will evaluate the continuation of the candidate in RSI training.

RAPID SEQUENCE INTUBATION
ASSESSMENT REPORT

NAME: EMPLOYEE NO:

ASSESSING CSO: DATE:

- Copy this form and give it to the Candidate for their records
- Remit the original to the Quality & Education Services Department
- Any category less than Proficient requires a re-assessment in that category only

ACCREDITATION ASSESSMENT ☐   RE-ASSESSMENT-1 ☐   RE-ASSESSMENT-2 ☐

ASSESSMENT CATEGORY FOR RSI	GRADE (MARK: X)		
	PROFICIENT	NEAR PROFICIENT	NOT PROFICIENT
THEORETICAL ASSESSMENT			
DRUG INFORMATION			
Question Group			
A ☐ B ☐ C ☐ D ☐ Questions			
ETCO$_2$ / CAPNOGRAPH			
Questions			
Waveform Recognition 8 waveforms			
One of the two devices to be assessed			
Novametrix CAPNOGRAPH – Bench top Demonstration			
ETCO$_2$ Connections			
Battery Changeover			
Screen Recognition			
Reset to Default Settings			
Amend Factory Settings			
Amend Alarm Settings			
MRx CAPNOGRAPH – Bench top Demonstration			
ETCO$_2$ Connections			
Connect SpO$_2$			
Battery Changeover			
Screen display			
Amend Alarm Settings			
PRACTICAL ASSESSMENT			
RSI SCENARIOS			
RSI – Preparation & Sections A			
Procedure B			
C			
D			
RSI - Difficult / Failed Sections A			
Intubation Drill B			
C			

COMMENTS:

CSO NAME & SIGNATURE

QUESTION	PERFORMANCE CRITERIA
A. Why has the $ETCO_2$ capnograph been authorised for use on MICA?	
B. What are normal $ETCO_2$ values?	
C. What are some of the physiological factors that would increase $ETCO_2$?	
D. What are some physiological factors that would decrease $ETCO_2$?	
E. What do the terms Capnography and Capnometry mean?	

IDENTIFY THE FOLLOWING WAVEFORMS OR IDENTIFIED COMPONENTS THEREOF

- ➤ A – Normal Waveform
  - A – B
  - B – C
  - C – D
  - D
  - D – E

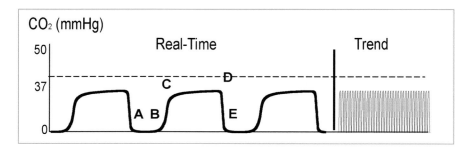

- ➤ B –

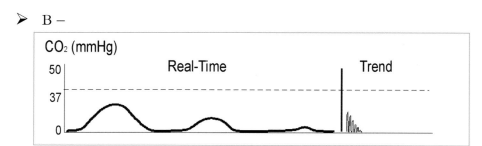

➢ C –

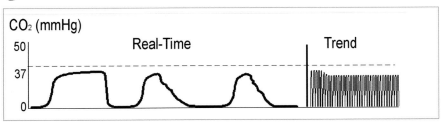

➢ D –

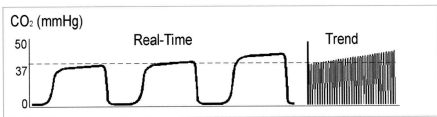

➢ E –

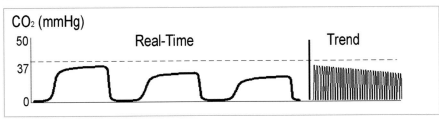

➢ F –

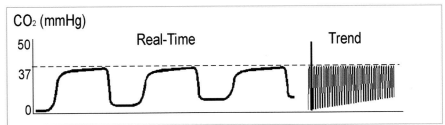

➤ G –

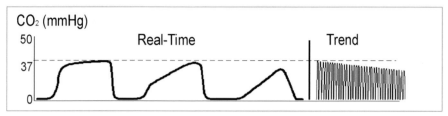

➤ H –

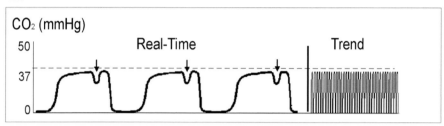

➤ I –

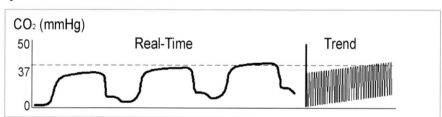

RAPID SEQUENCE INTUBATION ASSESSMENT – BENCH TOP DEMONSTRATION OF NOVAMETRIX CAPNOGRAPH

ASSESSMENT INSTRUCTIONS

Candidates are to demonstrate the following using a Novametrix Tidal Wave Sp Capnograph.

Proficient = ability to perform the task
Not Proficient = inability to perform the task

In this category the Performance Criteria is an assessment guide rather than an item-by-item assessment standard.

Connect ETCO$_2$

1. Select new Single patient airway adapter.
2. Ensure airway adapter is positioned vertically and located so that patient secretions and condensate water will flow away from the adapter's window not through or into it.
3. Snap Capnostat CO$_2$ sensor onto the airway adaptor.
4. Capnogram (CO$_2$ waveform) or ETCO$_2$ trend ETCO$_2$ values, and respiratory rate should be displayed on the monitor.

Connect SpO$_2$

1. Plug the connector into the end panel SpO$_2$ sensor input. The sensor connector is keyed to fit into the input in only one direction.
2. Gently squeeze the grips at the rear of the sensor.
3. Position fingertip against placement guide with fingernail toward the red light.
4. Release the finger grips.

Removing and Installing the Battery

1. Grasp the finger grips on each end of the battery cover.
2. Squeeze together and pull so that the cover opens to reveal the internal battery.
3. Remove the battery from the monitor.

The battery is keyed so that it can only be installed in one way. Make sure that the battery cover is properly closed before operating the monitor.

Screen Recognition

1. Using the Page key, scroll through and recognise the six display screens.
2. Data screen, $ETCO_2$ Waveform screen, Plethysmogram screen, $ETCO_2$ screen, SpO_2 trend screen, Respiratory screen.

Resetting to Factory Default Settings

1. Turn monitor off.
2. Press alarm and back light keys simultaneously.
3. Press power key, and turn monitor on.

Amend Factory Configuration Settings

1. Ensure $ETCO_2$ waveform screen is set.
2. Turn monitor off, then on.
3. Press adapter and backlight keys simultaneously.
4. Scroll through options and select preferred selections.

Amend Alarm Settings

1. Turn monitor on.
2. Press alarm key.
3. Press set alerts.
4. Scroll through options and select preferred selections.

ASSESSMENT INSTRUCTIONS

Candidates are to demonstrate the following using a Phillips MRx Monitor with Capnograph.

Proficient = ability to perform the task
Not Proficient = inability to perform the task

In this category the Performance Criteria is an assessment guide rather than an item–by–item assessment standard.

Connect ETCO$_2$

1. Identify CO_2 inlet on left side of MRx.
2. Ensure 'Filter Line' tubing is twisted to secure in position.
3. Connect to airway circuit.
4. Capnogram (CO_2 waveform) or ETCO$_2$ values, and respiratory rate should be displayed.

Connect SpO$_2$

1. Plug the connector into the end panel SpO$_2$ sensor input. The sensor connector is keyed to fit into the input in only one direction.
2. Gently squeeze the grips at the rear of the sensor.
3. Position fingertip against placement guide with fingernail toward the red light.
4. Release the finger grips.

Removing and Installing the Battery

1. Grasp the finger grips on each side of the battery.
2. Squeeze together and remove battery.
3. Reinsert fresh battery.

Screen Display

1. Using the menu key, select Displayed Waves.
2. Select Wave 3.
3. Identify and select CO_2.

Amend Alarm Settings

1. Using the menu key, select Measurements / Alarms.
2. Identify and select CO_2.
3. Select $ETCO_2$ limits.
4. Adjust Upper $ETCO_2$ limit.
5. Adjust Lower $ETCO_2$ limit.

RAPID SEQUENCE INTUBATION
ASSESSMENT – SCENARIOS

The aim of these scenarios is to assess proficiency in Rapid Sequence Intubation. If during the scenario other skills are revealed to be deficient the candidate may not necessarily fail this assessment. These associated skills are assessed only to the point where they provide a context for the assessment of rapid sequence intubation skill.

ASSESSMENT INSTRUCTIONS

This assessment has two scenarios, subdivided into seven sections, as follows;

➢ Rapid Sequence Intubation – Preparation & Procedure
- Section A – Initial Approach
- Section B – Preparation
- Section C – Rapid Sequence Intubation
- Section D – Patient Movement and Re-assessment

➢ Rapid Sequence Intubation – Difficult / Failed Intubation Drill
- Section A – Difficult / Failed ETT attempt
- Section B – Laryngeal Mask Airway
- Section C – Cricothyroidotomy

EQUIPMENT REQUIREMENTS
- A Self Inflating Bag Valve Mask Ventilator
- A Resuscitation Manikin that can be ventilated
- An Intravenous cannula simulation arm
- Novametrix Capnograph
- Phillips MRx Cardiac monitor, (with $ETCO_2$ and SpO_2 Monitoring as an alternative to the Novametrix Capnograph)
- Intubation equipment including, Laryngoscope, Blades, ETT, Bougie, LMA, Rapid Trac Kit (MICA airway bag)
- Correct placement equipment, ODD syringe, Stethoscope
- Drugs & Syringes
- Intravenous cannulation and fluid consumables

RAPID SEQUENCE INTUBATION SCENARIO ASSESSMENT FORM

The RSI Scenario Assessment Form has the following components:

- A running sequence of the Skills and Procedures.
- Feedback information to the candidate at intervals.
- Performance Criteria items that are required to be achieved for each Skill or Procedure.
- Marking section.
- Comments section.

CANDIDATE FEEDBACK INFORMATION SECTION

During the course of the scenario the assessor gives this information to the candidate as it relates to the sequence of the skills and procedures. Information provided directly to the candidate is in *italics*. Desired requirements are in normal text.

PERFORMANCE CRITERIA

All Performance Criteria items for each skill or procedure are to be achieved. If not, then proficiency isn't attained and this is to be marked accordingly on the RSI Scenario Assessment Form.

PASS CRITERIA

The candidate must achieve proficiency in all the Skills and Procedures and in accordance to the sequence on the assessment form. If the candidate deviates from the sequence and the Assessor deems it a legitimate deviation, please make comment on the Assessment Summary form. A deviation can only be deemed legitimate if the following principles are met:

- Patient resuscitation wasn't compromised.
- Rescuer or bystanders weren't put in danger.
- Preparatory steps and criteria were complete.
- Skill or Procedure Performance Criteria were still met.
- The deviation was not performed through lack of knowledge (i.e. the candidate is unable to clinically rationalise the deviation).

RAPID SEQUENCE INTUBATION SCENARIO ASSESSMENT FORM   RSI SCENARIO ONE – PREPARATION & PROCEDURE

CANDIDATE'S NAME: EMP. NO: DATE:

SKILL / PROCEDURE Expected sequence of action.	CANDIDATE FEEDBACK INFORMATION (I) Or REQUIREMENTS	PERFORMANCE CRITERIA To pass a skill or procedure, all performance criteria must be accomplished.	X: Not achieved ★	COMMENTS / SKILLS REQUIRING FOLLOW UP
SECTION A – INITIAL APPROACH				
BRIEF THE CANDIDATE	*You begin the scenario as the senior member of a MICA crew* *Action all BLS skills as required*			
BEGIN THE SCENARIO				
APPROACH	*You have been dispatched to a 25-year-old male patient involved in a high-speed motorcycle accident. The patient has come off his bike at approximately 60 kph and was not wearing a helmet*			
UNIVERSAL PRECAUTIONS		Indicates awareness to universal precautions.	★	
PRIMARY SURVEY	*No Dangers* *Some verbal & motor responses obvious (GCS 8)* *Airway clear* *Breathing present* *Difficult ventilation – trismus, snoring respirations, unable to insert OPA* *Pulse present* *No external haemorrhage*	Check for all primary survey areas Attempted ventilation with 100% oxygen	★	
VITAL SIGNS	*Pulse – 110 min, BP 115 / 75 mmHg, RR 22, GCS 8 (Eyes 2,Voice 2, Motor 4) Monitor – Sinus Tachycardia*	Full assessment of physiological status		
CERVICAL COLLAR		Appropriate size and application technique		

SKILL / PROCEDURE Expected sequence of action.	CANDIDATE FEEDBACK INFORMATION (I) Or REQUIREMENTS	PERFORMANCE CRITERIA To pass a skill or procedure, all performance criteria must be accomplished.	X: Not achieved ★	COMMENTS / SKILLS REQUIRING FOLLOW UP
SECTION B – PREPARATION				
DECISION MADE TO RSI PATIENT – Head injured patient, GCS <10 and difficult ventilation				
PRE-OXYGENATE PATIENT		Manual airway control & ventilation 100% oxygen & ventilation (Preferably Air Viva) Rate 12 min – Tidal Volume 10 ml /kg	★	
EQUIPMENT LAYOUT	Monitor	Able to be viewed by both officers.	★	
	ETCO$_2$ (CWI to come)	Turn on, check it is working (gently blow through adaptor)	★	
	SpO$_2$	Connect SpO$_2$ to patient and commence monitoring SpO$_2$ & heart rate Look for change in SpO$_2$	★	
TASK ALLOCATION & SCENE LEADERSHIP	Scene manager is the senior RSI qualified MICA paramedic who will manage ETT/ Airway	Senior RSI qualified MP will prepare and check advanced airway equipment Allocate / identify airway assistant, initiate pre-oxygenation and cricoid pressure Allocate / identify drug assistant, initiate drawing up, checks, identification Allocate / identify IV fluid assistant, initiate preparation	★	
ENDOTRACHEAL INTUBATION EQUIPMENT	All equipment sourced and arranged in accessible manner	2 – Laryngoscopes (or 1 handle & 2 blades) ETT + 1 size down ETT tape or securing device 10 ml syringe (and connected to ETT??) Introducer, Bougie ODD device Stethoscope, Orogastric Tube	★	
LARYNGEAL MASK AIRWAY	All equipment sourced and arranged in accessible manner	Correct size LMA KY Gel 50ml syringe	★	
CRICOTHYROIDOTOMY KIT	Sourced and arranged in accessible manner	Cricothyroidotomy kit preparation Identify Cricoid Membrane / Draw Line across.	★	

SKILL / PROCEDURE Expected sequence of action.	CANDIDATE FEEDBACK INFORMATION (I) Or REQUIREMENTS	PERFORMANCE CRITERIA To pass a skill or procedure, all performance criteria must be accomplished.	X: Not achieved ⋆	COMMENTS / SKILLS REQUIRING FOLLOW UP
FUNCTIONAL INTRAVENOUS ACCESS	Appropriate sized cannula and IV Fluid solution arranged.	Large Gauge IV Cannula (Forearm preferably) Free flowing bag of Hartmann's Solution Use of 3 way Tap at cannula site and Reflux Valve in IV line Fluid load prior to RSI (10 ml / kg) 500 ml fluid load at least If Blood Pressure falls at any time it is to be treated with vigorous fluid resuscitation @ 20 mls / kg as per CPG	⋆	2 IV's preferably
DRUG PREPARATION	Sedation Drugs prior • Midazolam (2.5, 5, 7.5, 10) • Fentanyl (50, 100) Paralysing Agents • Suxamethonium (75, 100, 125, 150) Sedation • Bolus • Maintenance Infusion Atropine – if required as per CPG (HR < 60) *Patient 80 kg* *Pulse 110 / min.* *BP 115 / 75* *GCS 8*	Correct drug preparation, dosages, syringes and identification thereof Assess patient weight. Midazolam 15 mg & 20 ml syringe Fentanyl 100mcg &10 ml syringe Suxamethonium 100 mg & 3 ml syringe @ 2 Morphine & Midazolam Infusion 30mg of each drug into a 50 ml syringe @ 5 – 10 ml / hour Atropine 0.6 mg in 1 ml syringe	⋆	
SECTION C – RAPID SEQUENCE INTUBATION				
HEAD POSITION & LARYNGOSCOPY	Apply correct head position	Neutral Head position Undo Cx Collar Manual in-line traction / stabilisation of head	⋆	

SKILL / PROCEDURE Expected sequence of action.	CANDIDATE FEEDBACK INFORMATION (I) Or REQUIREMENTS	PERFORMANCE CRITERIA To pass a skill or procedure, all performance criteria must be accomplished.		X: Not achieved	COMMENTS / SKILLS REQUIRING FOLLOW UP

DRUG ADMINISTRATION	Sedation and paralysis agents administered	Gentle Cricoid pressure
		Administer
		   Fentanyl 50 mcg IVI
		   Midazolam 0.05 mg / kg (4.0mg) IVI
		   Suxamethonium 1.5 mg / kg (125mg) IVI
			*		

LARYNGOSCOPY	Proceed with cricoid pressure and laryngoscopy	Wait 30 – 60 seconds Look for jaw relaxation, do not rely on fasciculations Firm cricoid pressure – after paralysis Appropriate Laryngoscopy technique Grade laryngeal view – 1 to 4	*		

ENDOTRACHEAL INTUBATION, CHECKS	Proceed with endotracheal intubation and confirm position	Direct assistant to read SpO$_2$ and HR values
		Standard ETT Checks
		   Cord visualisation, ETT Misting
		   ODD Test, Inflate, Auscultation, Squash Test
		   ETCO$_2$
		Secure ETT in position
		Oropharyngeal airway
			*		ODD – if oesophagus intubation indicated, connect ETCO$_2$ @ 6 breaths and re-assess ETCO$_2$ reading.
					If ETCO$_2$ satisfactory leave ETT in-situ, if not remove.
					(Looking at effectiveness of ODD – must record on PCR)

POST ENDOTRACHEAL INTUBATION CHECKS & MANAGEMENT	*ETCO$_2$ – 40 mmHg / waveform normal* *SpO$_2$ – 95 %* *BP 85 / 60 mmHg* *Pulse 130 / min*	Look for ETCO$_2$ waveform. Do not 'chase' numbers (desirable ETCO$_2$ – 30-35 mmHg) Appropriate ventilation – Rate 12/ min, Tidal Volume @ 10 ml / kg Correct hypotension immediately – IV Fluid load @ 20 ml / Kg Cervical Collar – ETT protection	*		
POST ETT SEDATION	Sedation and additional paralysis agents Pancuronium	Pancuronium 8 mg & 5 ml syringe Bolus Midazolam if required (2.5 – 5 mg) Morphine & Midazolam Infusion 5 – 10 mg per hour (5 – 10 ml / hr) Label Infusions – if used Orogastric tube at opportunity	*		

SKILL / PROCEDURE Expected sequence of action.	CANDIDATE FEEDBACK INFORMATION (I) Or REQUIREMENTS	PERFORMANCE CRITERIA To pass a skill or procedure, all performance criteria must be accomplished.	X: Not achieved	COMMENTS / SKILLS REQUIRING FOLLOW UP
SECTION D – PATIENT MOVEMENT & REASSESSMENT				

PATIENT TRANSFER	Move patient
	Reconfirm ETT position
		Plan / allocate tasks for movement
		   Pre-oxygenate
		   Disconnect ETT
		   Controlled move
		   Re-oxygenate
		   Reconfirm ETT position
		   Standard ETT checks
		   ETT Misting, Auscultation
		   $ETCO_2$
			★	

POST PATIENT MOVEMENT	Reconfirm ETT position Vital Signs $ETCO_2 - 35\ mm\ Hg$ $SpO_2 - 97\ \%$ $HR\ 110/\ min$ $BP\ 125\ /\ 85\ mm\ Hg$	Standard ETT Checks ETT Misting, Auscultation $ETCO_2$ SpO_2 Pulse & BP Check	★	
PATIENT RE-ASSESSMENT	Continual re-assessment for indicators of inadequate sedation, paralysis or adverse physiological trend from other causes. *Observations remain stable*	Verbalises the following; Regular check of $ETCO_2$ waveform and value Regular check of cardiovascular status Regular check of respiratory status Regular check for clinical indicators for inadequate sedation or paralysis	★	

END OF SCENARIO ONE

RAPID SEQUENCE INTUBATION SCENARIO ASSESSMENT FORM   RSI SCENARIO TWO – DIFFICULT / FAILED INTUBATION

CANDIDATE'S NAME: EMP. NO: DATE:

SKILL / PROCEDURE Expected sequence of action.	CANDIDATE FEEDBACK INFORMATION (I) Or REQUIREMENTS	PERFORMANCE CRITERIA To pass a skill or procedure, all performance criteria must be accomplished.	X: Not achieved ★	COMMENTS / SKILLS REQUIRING FOLLOW UP
SECTION A – FAILED ETT ATTEMPT				
BRIEF THE CANDIDATE	*You begin the scenario as the senior member of a MICA crew.* *The scenario begins at the point of ETT insertion from Scenario Nos 1*			
BEGIN THE SCENARIO				
ENDOTRACHEAL INTUBATION, CHECKS & FAILED INTUBATION DRILL	Proceed with intubation *You are unable to visualise the vocal cords* *You are unable to ventilate patient*	Direct assistant to read ETCO$_2$ and HR values Oropharyngeal or Nasopharyngeal airway Manual airway control & ventilation Rate 12 / min, Tidal Volume 10 ml / kg Re-oxygenate patient – 30 to 60 seconds & guided by SpO$_2$	★	
RE-ATTEMPT ENDOTRACHEAL INTUBATION WITH PLASTIC AIRWAY BOUGIE & CHECKS	Re-attempt endotracheal intubation with assistance of Bougie Attempt to confirm position. *Standard test inconclusive* *No ETCO$_2$ waveform* *SpO$_2$ values dropping*	Use smaller size ETT Use of Bougie Maximum 30 seconds in attempt or desaturation Attempt to confirm ETT position Standard ETT checks Cord visualisation, ETT Misting, ODD Test, Inflate, Auscultation, Squash Test ETCO$_2$ Return to oropharyngeal or nasopharyngeal airway, manual airway control and ventilation. Re-oxygenate patient	★	ODD – if oesophagus intubation indicated, connect ETCO$_2$ @ 6+ breaths and re-assess ETCO$_2$ reading. If ETCO$_2$ satisfactory leave ETT in-situ, if not remove. (Looking at effectiveness of ODD – must record on PCR)

SKILL / PROCEDURE Expected sequence of action.	CANDIDATE FEEDBACK INFORMATION (I) Or REQUIREMENTS	PERFORMANCE CRITERIA To pass a skill or procedure, all performance criteria must be accomplished.	★	X: Not achieved	COMMENTS / SKILLS REQUIRING FOLLOW UP
SECTION B – LARYNGEAL MASK AIRWAY					

LARYNGEAL MASK AIRWAY &
CHECKS
	Insert LMA
	
	Conformation checks inconclusive
	SpO₂ values dropping
	
	You are unable to ventilate patient.
		LMA Preparation
		Correct insertion technique
		Placement confirmation checks
		    Auscultation
		    Chest rise and fall
		Return to oropharyngeal or nasopharyngeal airway, manual airway control and ventilation
		Re-oxygenate patient
			★		

SECTION C – CRICOTHYROIDOTOMY					
CRICOTHYROIDOTOMY & CHECKS	Insert Cricothyroidotomy and proceed to ventilate patient	Cricothyroidotomy Kit Preparation Insertion as per CWI Confirm correct placement Secure correctly as per CWI Re-oxygenate patient, using Jet ventilation technique Prepare for paralysing agent to wear off	★		

END OF SCENARIO TWO

Twenty questions are to be asked to test knowledge and understanding of the drugs used in the RSI process. Questions are asked about all drugs used in the RSI process.

All questions are drawn from the information contained in the MICA Continuing Professional Education on RSI handouts, the AV Clinical Practice Guidelines, and the RSI reference book (3rd Edition). Ensure you refer to the current version of the AV CPGs.

Select Question Paper A, B, C or D and indicate on the Assessment Report which paper has been used. If this is a re-assessment, select a different paper to which has been used previously.

To attain proficiency, the candidate must correctly answer 18 or more of the 20 questions (i.e., 90%).

NOTES